I0804192

CHRISTIAN LIVING

Gender and Sexuality

Biblical Sanity in a World of Confusion

MICHAEL RICCARDI

CLC
PUBLICATIONS
Fort Washington, PA 19034

Gender and Sexuality: Biblical Sanity in a World of Confusion
The Christian Life Series

Published by CLC Publications

USA: P.O. Box 1449, Fort Washington, PA 19034
www.clcpublications.com

UK: Kingsway CLC Trust
Unit 5, Glendale Avenue, Sandycroft, Flintshire, CH5 2QP
www.equippingthechurch.com

ISBN (paperback): 978-1-61958-392-4
ISBN (ebook): 978-1-61958-397-9

Printed in the United States of America

Italics in Scripture quotations, if not original to the NASB, are the emphasis of the author.

Contents

PRAISE FOR
GENDER AND SEXUALITY

"As our culture increasingly rebels against God's good design for men and women, we must understand and affirm and celebrate God's brilliant design. Mike Riccardi helps us do that with his timely, clear, insightful, and sound teaching."

— Andy Naselli, professor of systematic theology and New Testament,
Bethlehem College and Seminary
One of the pastors of The North Church

"In *Gender and Sexuality*, Mike Riccardi has issued a theological clarion call to the evangelical church to understand and respond biblically to the existential threat posed—both to society and the church—by the gender ideology movement in all its demonic shapes and forms. Gender ideology is a matter about which the church must be equipped to engage the culture. Why? Because, as Riccardi explains, "Precious people, made in the image of God, are the collateral damage of the transgender cult." *Gender and Sexuality* is a must-read for every Christian apologist—and every Christian is to be an apologist (1 Pet 3:15)."

— Darrell Harrison
Host, *Just Thinking* podcast

"It is refreshing to read a book about human sexuality that realizes the unbreakable connection between nature and grace. The main reason many modern Christians have been led astray on the issues imbedded in gender and sexuality stems from the failure to realize that the God of grace is the God of nature. In the beginning this one true God created mankind to consist of men and women, each with different, innate qualities and responsibilities. It is through a recognition of this divine design that men and women can live fulfilled, meaningful lives. Only through the fulfillment of this natural design can the revelation of God's grace in Jesus Christ be displayed. Mike Riccardi understands this and guides readers through the teaching of Scripture so that we can clearly understand it, too. He does so with a pastoral sensitivity that shows the hope of the gospel for sinners, including those who have misconstrued human sexuality and, as a result, have been living in rebellion to their Creator. This book deserves a wide readership and is a welcome ally in the important and necessary work of recovering biblical truth regarding men, women, sexuality, and gender. I highly recommend it."

— Tom Ascol
Pastor, Grace Baptist Church, Cape Coral, Florida
President, Founders Ministries
President, Institute of Public Theology

Titles in the Christian Life Series

Published in 2023

Heaven and Hell: A Survey of the Biblical Doctrines of Personal Eschatology (Kevin Zuber)

The Forgotten Attributes of God: God's Nature and Why It Matters (Peter Sammons)

Old Testament Survey I: Genesis to Esther (Nathan LeMaster)

Well Done: A Strategy for Life Stewardship (Reagan Rose)

Becoming a Worthy Reader: How to Read and Study the Bible (Kevin Zuber)

Published in 2024

New Testament Survey I: Matthew to Acts & Johannine Literature (Nathan LeMaster)

Gender and Sexuality (Michael Riccardi)

Coming in 2025 (tentative titles)

The Church and Church Membership (John MacArthur)

Old Testament Survey II (Nathan LeMaster)

Salvation and Sanctification (author TBD)

The Spiritual Disciplines (author TBD)

Coming in 2026 and beyond (tentative titles)

Spiritual Leadership (author TBD)

The Creeds of the Church (author TBD)

New Testament Survey II (Nathan LeMaster)

Spiritual Gifts and Service (author TBD)

The Person of God or *The Authority of Scripture* (author TBD)

Biblical Reconciliation (author TBD)

Marriage and Family Counseling (author TBD)

Discipling and Mentoring (author TBD)

Global and Local Missions (author TBD)

Series Foreword

The Christian Life Series

From the time the Lord called me to Grace Community Church, I have had two primary goals: to preach the Word of God faithfully (2 Tim. 4:2) and to entrust the truth to faithful men (2:2). In keeping with those priorities, The Master's Seminary has played a key role in training future pastors to handle the Word accurately and defend its truth boldly. These Master's men have gone out to serve and shepherd churches across the nation and around the world.

Several years ago, to assist these faithful pastors in their shepherding work, the seminary created a lay-training program, comprised of online video courses. The Institute for the Christian Life is designed to train lay people in four fundamental categories: Bible Knowledge, Sound Doctrine, Christian Living, and Shepherding Care, bringing biblical training, theological instruction, and practical ministry into the pew and the living room—making these indispensable tools accessible to believers at all levels of spiritual maturity and church leadership. This book series complements those online courses, as an aid for small group discussion and individual study.

My prayer for you as you read this book is that you would grow in the grace and knowledge of the Lord Jesus Christ. As the apostle Paul expressed in Ephesians 1:18–19, "*I pray* that the eyes of your heart may be enlightened, so that you will know what is the hope of His calling, what are the riches of the glory of His inheritance in the saints, and what is the surpassing greatness of His power toward us who believe."

John MacArthur
Pastor, Grace Community Church, Sun Valley, California
Chancellor, The Master's University and Seminary

Editorial Preface

Dr. Mike Riccardi (PhD, The Master's Seminary) serves as Assistant Professor of Theology at The Master's Seminary and Pastor of Evangelism and Outreach at Grace Community Church where he also shepherds the fellowship group GraceLife.

In a noisy world of conflicting ideologies and blurred lines, this book stands as a clarion call to address one of the most crucial issues of our time—the distortion of human identity in contemporary Western culture. *Gender and Sexuality: Biblical Sanity in a World of Confusion* fearlessly navigates the tumultuous waters of anthropological discourse, revealing an urgent need to return to the foundational truths that define who we are as human beings.

Dr. Riccardi boldly confronts the prevailing confusion surrounding the doctrine of anthropology, emphasizing the pivotal role of understanding man's nature while also untangling the complex challenges Christians face in a world turned upside down. The book contends that men and women are not autonomous self-creators but divine creations, designed in the image of a loving God, who desires that we live in harmony with His commands.

Dr. Riccardi examines the complementary roles of men and women while confronting topics such as homosexuality, transgenderism, and gender roles, courageously challenging the prevailing narratives in mainstream society. He shows that genuine love lies not in embracing false notions but in declaring the transformative power of the gospel, the sure path to true sanctification.

Prepare to have your convictions challenged, your perspectives reshaped, and your understanding of true humanity deepened. More than a book, *Gender and Sexuality* is a powerful proclamation that beckons us to rediscover the profound beauty of our God-given identities and reclaim the essence of what it means to be truly human.

An editorial note to the reader: In light of the topics being covered in this book, please be aware that this book often uses traditional words and phrases related to gender, such as "man" as a gender-inclusive term. This wording is in line with the New American Standard Bible (1995), the Bible translation used throughout the book.

Peter Sammons, PhD, Series Editor
Author of *Reprobation and God's Sovereignty*
and *The Forgotten Attributes of God*

Introduction

WHAT'S WRONG WITH the world today? Specifically, what is wrong with the thinking of contemporary western culture? The answer to those questions could fill volumes, to be sure. But if I had to identify one area of inquiry—one of the ten traditional doctrinal loci of systematic theology—I would pick the doctrine of anthropology, the doctrine of man. What is man? Who in the world is he? Is man an animal, evolved from goo? Is he a creature made in the image of God, and so, therefore, accountable to God? Not only that, but what is *a* man? What is *a* woman? We are so far down the path of God's judgment as a society that we can no longer define the most basic tenets of our own human identity.

A Downward Spiral of Divine Judgment

John MacArthur has so often spoken of the progression of divine judgment that Paul laid out in Romans 1. After a nation abandons God (1:18–23), God abandons that nation and leaves the nation to self-destruct in the fulfillment of the citizens' own wicked desires.

As a result, there is first a sexual revolution, in which "God [gives] them over in the lusts of their hearts to impurity, so that their bodies would be dishonored among them" (1:24). Second, there is a homosexual revolution, in which "God [gives] them over to degrading passions," namely, "their women exchang[e] the natural function for that which is unnatural, and in the same way also the men abando[n] the natural function of the woman and bur[n] in their desire toward one another, men with men committing indecent acts" (1:26–27).

Finally, there is the judgment of the depraved (or reprobate) mind, which results in doing "those things which are not proper" (1:28). The reprobate mind is a mind that doesn't function, so much so that it's a point of controversy to insist that men are men and are not women, and that women are women and are not men.

Transgenderism is the last stop of corruption for a society that has given itself over to wanton sexual license—fornication, adultery, and the eventual abortion that kills the children who are conceived as a result of that sexual boundlessness; the desecration of marriage in widespread toleration and celebration of divorce; and the redefinition and destruction of marriage by the embrace of homosexuality.

The Polluted Fountain: Self-Deification

It's important to understand what's behind all of this. From rampant sexual immorality (and abortion on demand, which makes it practical), to homosexualism and the desecration of marriage, all the way to transgenderism—it all stems from the same polluted fountain: our culture's attempt at self-deification. In the garden, Satan tempted Adam and Eve to rebel against God by holding out to them the deceitful promise that they would become like God in their rebellion (Gen. 3:5), and our society is intoxicated with the very same prospect. They want to be God.

What do I mean? Well, when Jesus affirmed the creation-reality that in the beginning, God created mankind in His own image as male and female (Matt. 19:4; Gen. 1:27), He affirmed that the Creator's intent was for gender to be binary and immutable, and that such order—even amidst unity in diversity—reflects His own character and nature. However, transgenderism preaches, "No, God is not who determines your gender and identity; you are. You create male and female in *your* image. You do what feels right for you, and don't let anybody—least of all your Creator—tell you differently."

In the same text, when Jesus referenced humankind being created male and female, He underscored that the Creator of marriage and of mankind defined marriage to be a lifelong covenant between one man and one woman (Matt. 19:4–5; Gen. 2:24; Mal. 2:14–16). Scripture's condemnation of homosexuality in Scripture could not be clearer (Gen. 18–19; Lev. 18:22; 20:13; Rom. 1:26–27; 1 Cor. 6:9–11; 1 Tim. 1:9–10). However, the vehement homosexualism of our society declares, "No, God will not dictate to us what marriage is or is not. We will define marriage any way we see fit."

In the same vein, because God has created mankind uniquely in His image (Gen. 1:27), all human life is sacred. That's why the one who sheds man's blood will have his own blood shed: "For in the image of God He made man" (Gen. 9:6). Murder is such a distortion of the image of God that a murderer is required to pay for that offense with his own life. God

Himself is the Creator of all life. However, the culture of death, prostituting the cause of women's rights to satisfy its own bloodlust, pronounces, "No, that is not a child in the womb but a fetus, just a clump of cells that isn't a human person until the mother feels like it's a living human person."[1] If the mother doesn't want her child, she may hire a skilled hitman to murder the unborn baby. But if she does declare the child is a person, her friends will throw her a baby shower.

The common thread is the exaltation of self in the place of God. You are the one who determines your identity, not God your Creator. You define marriage, not God the Creator of marriage. You determine life and personhood, not God the Creator of all life. Sexual immorality, abortion, homosexualism, and transgenderism are our society's fledgling attempts at self-deification—the creature's rebellious hallucination that he is Creator and Lord. God declares that He creates male and female, reveals gender in biology, and establishes norms of masculinity and femininity. He creates marriage and defines it for humanity, and He ascribes value to all His image-bearers.

Man protests, "No, He doesn't. We do that for ourselves."

This is little more than the rebellious complaint of the nobleman's slaves: "We will not have this [God] to reign over us" (Luke 19:14, KJV).

Salt and Light

In undertaking to articulate the Bible's teaching on gender and sexuality, then, this book touches on an extremely relevant subject, given our current cultural moment. If anthropology is the battleground issue of our day, gender and sexuality may very well be the crux of the competing worldviews of Christianity and secularism.

It is no exaggeration to say the LGBTQ movement has hijacked our culture. The normalization and celebration of homosexual relationships in pop-culture—TV, music, and movies—is ever present. The educational system actively grooms children for sexual deviancy by introducing perverse sexual themes as early as kindergarten. The medical system pressures adults, and even children, to solve feelings of gender dysphoria by mutilating themselves with life-altering surgeries. The legal system is increasingly leveraged to bankrupt those who dare to dissent from this new sexual orthodoxy.

1 Steven Ertelt, "MSNBC Host: Life Begins When Parents Say It Does, Not Based on Science," https://www.lifenews.com/2013/07/23/msnbc-host-life-begins-when-parents-say-it-does-not-based-on-science (accessed December 2023).

If the people of Christ are going to have any hope of being salt and light amid the decay and darkness of this dying culture (Matt. 5:13–16), we must be equipped to confront this perverse sexual credo with a biblical doctrine of gender and sexuality—to proclaim the Lordship of Jesus Christ, and His right, as King of the universe, to define good and evil in His world.

Each week, as you depart from your churches (which, by God's good design, function as something of a haven for truth and holiness), you enter a world of chaos and corruption, a world that never stops vying for your allegiance. This world lies in the power of the evil one (1 John 5:19), who commands the spiritual forces of wickedness (Eph. 6:12) that labor to deceive the people of God, that seek to seduce you with fine-sounding arguments (Col. 2:4), even as the Serpent did with Eve.

The evil one and his cohorts seek to woo your thinking away from the simplicity and purity of devotion to Christ (2 Cor. 11:3), into the empty deception of the elementary principles of this world (Col. 2:8). And so, you must be equipped to stand against those attacks. Your minds must be prepared to resist those advances and to stand firm in the faith.

But you must not only play defense. You must also be equipped to confront the lies of the culture with the truth, tearing down strongholds, demolishing arguments raised up against the knowledge of God, and taking every thought captive to the obedience of Christ (2 Cor. 10:3–5).

You need not only to withstand the lies; you must confront the lies. You must bring the light of the truth into the darkness. You must bring the salt of heaven into the corruption of earth, boldly calling sinners to the repentance and faith that lays hold of Christ for righteousness and for eternal joy.

This book aims to serve you to those ends.

1

What Is Man?

The Foundation of Our Identity

As I PREPARED TO WRITE on biblical sexuality, I realized how central the notion of identity has become in this discussion. Our culture has actually conflated sexuality with identity. According to the world around us, we are defined by our sexual appetites. We are what we desire. If we ever act out of accord with our basest desires and impulses, we are somehow not "being true to our authentic self."

The following credo is fundamental to the errors addressed in his book—whether same-sex attraction, homosexuality, or transgenderism: "I am what I feel like I am. I may identify as whatever my feelings tell me I am, even if what I feel inside doesn't match the objective facts of the external world. I am who I say I am." That doesn't sound much different from what God told Moses at the burning bush: "I am who I am" (Exod. 3:14).

The problem with that is: That is not how Scripture defines humankind. God alone declares, "I am who I am," and man is not God.

The creature's ancient desire to depose the Creator and reign in His place is what expelled Lucifer from heaven, and it's the sin that lies at the heart of all sexual rebellion. Fundamentally, people conceive themselves to be something they are not: autonomous determiners of their own identity.

This means properly understanding our own sexuality is downstream of our identity at a more foundational level. Before we can properly answer, "With whom do I belong, sexually?" we must answer, "Who am I, most fundamentally?"

The Bible is to man what the owner's manual is to our cars: detailed instructions about what we are and how we are to function, direct from the One who created us and designed us. The chaos of the culture is the result of society's rejection of the Bible's answers to these questions. To cut through the chaos, we must return to Scripture's teaching on man's identity.

MAN IS A CREATURE

In the first sentence of the first chapter of John Calvin's magisterial classic, *The Institutes of the Christian Religion,* he famously wrote, "Nearly all the wisdom we possess, that is to say, true and sound wisdom, consists of two parts: the knowledge of God and of ourselves."[1] Our understanding of ourselves is inseparable from our understanding of who God is and how we relate to Him. Our identity is rooted in what God says we are.

It begins with the doctrine of creation. Our identity begins with the fact that we are not animals that have evolved from a primordial soup. Still less are we semi-divine demigods, free to be the masters of our fates and the captains of our souls. The very first thing to say about man—in fact, the very first thing that the Bible *does* say about man—is that he is a creature: "Then God said, 'Let Us make man in Our image. . . .' God created man in His own image, in the image of God He created him; male and female He created them" (Gen. 1:26–27). This is where our identity begins. "It is He who made us, and not we ourselves" (Ps. 100:3).

Most fundamentally, man is the direct creation of the Creator God. This means that we are not ultimate. We are accountable to the God who has made us. We look to Him to tell us who we are and how we must live.[2]

CREATION UNDER ATTACK

This is why the biblical doctrine of creation is always under attack. If you want to free man from his accountability to his Creator and the totalizing claims of the law of God so he can be left alone to sin in peace, you must start at the very root. You must seek to undermine the doctrine of creation.

---

1 John Calvin, *Institutes of the Christian Religion,* 2 vols., ed. John T. McNeill, trans. Ford Lewis Battles (Louisville, KY: Westminster John Knox Press, 1960), 1:35 (1.1.1).

2 Joel Beeke and Paul Smalley write, "The Bible roots our understanding of man in creation. Human life has purpose and meaning because we did not come into being by accident or by our own will, but by the will of God, who created both us and the world in which we live. Therefore, we belong to him and exist for him. . . . The doctrine of creation anchors our worldview in God, directs our lives to his glory, and protects us against idolatry" (Joel R. Beeke and Paul M. Smalley, *Reformed Systematic Theology*, Vol. 2 [Wheaton: Crossway, 2020], 55).

If there is no God, then humans aren't creatures accountable to their Creator. It is because of the denial of the biblical doctrine of creation that the world is in chaos today.

Of course, if we deny the doctrine of creation, we have an entire creation to explain away. It's a tall order to survey the glories of this world—every moment breathing in the blessings of a bountiful, personal Creator—while simultaneously denying that a Creator has created the creation you're living in and enjoying.

Thus, Satan has focused his attacks on the doctrine of creation itself. Because of this, many false theories of creation have arisen, which attempt to explain away the facts before our eyes. Many polytheistic accounts of creation exist, as in Greek mythology, in which the material creation is said to be the result of sexual reproduction or warfare among the gods.

Pantheistic accounts, as in Hinduism, erase the Creator-creature distinction and say that the creation is God, and God is the creation. This is popular in new-age neo-paganism, in which people personalize the inanimate universe (because they've denied the personal God who is) by saying something like, "The Universe is smiling upon us today."

Panentheistic accounts exist, which do not say that God *is* the creation, but that He is *in* every aspect of creation; God is the soul of the universe, and the physical creation is like His body.[3] This view also fails to maintain the Creator-creature distinction.

Finally, materialism claims that physical matter is all that exists. The universe is eternal, and there is no immaterial. Nothing was created; what we see just always was, in some form. This is the *a priori* assumption (dare we say, "unscientific presupposition") of atheism, Darwinism, neo-Darwinism, and any model that depends on the notion of a "Big Bang."

Uniting all those false theories is the worship of the creation at the expense of the worship of the Creator. Pantheism and panentheism ultimately call for the worship of the creature by failing to distinguish God's being from the creature's being. The creation is God; worship it. Materialism, having evacuated any place for an immaterial Creator-God from its worldview, in the absence of the true God makes the physical creation god. Since they don't acknowledge the true God, they make a god out of what there is.

This is such a testimony to the fundamentally religious nature of the heart of man. We are inveterate worshippers. We must worship something. And if you have a sin-fueled agenda to suppress the truth in unrighteousness

3 Beeke and Smalley, *Reformed Systematic Theology,* 2:58.

(as Rom. 1:18 says)—an *a priori* commitment to reject the biblical Creator because you don't want to be subject to His law—you do what Romans 1:23–25 says: you "exchange the glory of the incorruptible God . . . [to] worship and serve the creature rather than the Creator."

As Beeke and Smalley put it, "If the universe has no Creator, then *it* becomes our God."[4]

Six-Day Creation

But against all of that truth-suppression, Scripture testifies with uniformity, clarity, and authority that the one true God, the God of the Bible, has created all things by the word of His mouth in the span of six, literal, 24-hour days:

- Genesis 1:31–2:3: "God saw all that He had made, and behold, it was very good. And there was evening and there was morning, the sixth day. Thus the heavens and the earth were completed, and all their hosts. By the seventh day God completed His work which He had done, and He rested on the seventh day from all His work which He had done. Then God blessed the seventh day and sanctified it, because in it He rested from all His work which God had created and made."
- Exodus 20:11: "For in six days Yahweh made the heavens and the earth, the sea and all that is in them, and rested on the seventh day."
- Exodus 31:17: "It is a sign between Me and the sons of Israel forever; for in six days Yahweh made heaven and earth, but on the seventh day He ceased from labor, and was refreshed."
- Psalm 33:6, 9: "By the word of Yahweh the heavens were made, And by the breath of His mouth all their host. . . . For He spoke, and it was done; He commanded, and it stood fast" (Heb. 11:3).[5]
- Matthew 19:4: "And [Jesus] answered and said, 'Have you not read that He who created them from the beginning made them male and female'" If God made Adam and Eve "from the beginning" of creation, millions of years did not pass from the creation of the world to the creation of man.

---

4 Beeke, and Smalley, Reformed Systematic Theology, 2:60 (emphasis added).

5 The phrases "and it was done" (*wayyehi*) and "and it stood fast" (*wayya'amōd*) are *wayyiqtol* verb forms, precluding a lapse of time between God's creative action ("He spoke") and its effect ("it was done"). The grammar does not allow for interpreting that as, "He spoke, and millions of years passed, and then finally the evolutionary process yielded stars and fish and creeping things." No, He spoke, and immediately upon His speaking, it was done. This does not allow for an old earth.

- Luke 11:49–51: "Some of them they will kill and some they will persecute, so that the blood of all the prophets, shed since the foundation of the world, may be charged against this generation, from the blood of Abel to the blood of Zechariah . . . " Jesus here considers the murder of Abel in Genesis 4 to have happened at "the foundation of the world," not thousands or millions of years after the world was founded.

If we are to have any hope of confronting the lies of our culture with the truth of human identity—first of all as the direct creation of God—we must steadfastly insist upon Scripture's teaching of six-day creation. Those two issues are inextricably linked; they stand and fall together.

If the Bible doesn't mean what it says when it claims that God created the world in six days, no consistent basis exists upon which we can insist that the Bible means what it says when it claims that God created humans as male and female and that male and female are fixed and unchangeable categories. That's why, if you say you believe in a six-day creation, you will get laughed out of every classroom, newsroom, and break room you walk into. The natural man must scoff at this most basic, fundamental claim if he is going to create his own identity and live according to his own morality.

But against all of that, let it be heard with clarity: This is your identity, dear reader. You are not an evolved animal, nor a slave to your own basest passions and impulses. Neither are you a mini-god, unaccountable to anyone but yourself, fabricating your own "truth," or speaking your own identity into existence. You are, most fundamentally, a creature, and so you are accountable to God your Creator, subject to the identity He has given you, subject to the law of His mouth as the rule of your life.

You must order your life as He says you must, under the Lordship of His Son, Jesus Christ. If you don't, you must suffer the consequences of divine justice—both in this life, in which the way of the transgressor is hard (Prov. 13:15, KJV), and in the life to come, in which judgment will be righteously poured out on all who do not bow the knee to Christ (Matt. 25:41).

Man is an Image Bearer

But man is not just a creature. Man is a creature made in God's image. The next most fundamental concept concerning man's identity is that he is created as the image of God. That is the second designation Scripture uses to describe man: "Let Us make man in Our image, according to Our likeness" (Gen. 1:26); "God created man in His own image, in the image of God He created him" (Gen. 1:27; Gen. 5:1, 3; 9:6; 1 Cor. 11:7; James 3:9).

A study of the terms for "image" (*tselem; eikōn*) and "likeness" (*demuth; homoiosis*) leads to the conclusion that the terms express representation and similarity. For "image," one trustworthy resource says, "In the ancient world, a king or a ruler would place an image or idol of himself in his realm to symbolize his sovereignty there. When others saw the image, they knew who had control. [In the same way], God's image bearers represent God in the world" (e.g., Num. 33:52; 2 Kings 11:18).[6] And a "likeness" was simply a pattern after an original (e.g., 2 Kings 16:10; 2 Chron. 5:3), something like the original but not identical to it. Genesis 5:3 explained that Seth was made in Adam's likeness, which meant that Seth was like Adam in that he was a human being from Adam's loins, even while he was not identical to Adam.

Thus, man is not identical to God, as pantheism teaches, nor a part of God, as in panentheism. We do not partake in God's incommunicable attributes; God alone is eternal and infinite, while man is temporal and finite. Man's creation in the image of God does not mean we creatures are so much like our Creator as to be gods in any sense. Instead, being created in the image of God means we are like God in very important ways; we do partake in His communicable attributes to varying degrees.

We also are created to represent God in the world in a way that is unique among the other creatures. In fact, it's best to say not that man *has* the image of God somewhere dwelling within him, but that man *is* the image of God on earth, representing God to the world.

Why are we here? What is the purpose of our lives? What am I supposed to do in this world? Just as sinful men make idols—images—of their gods, that they might worship a visual expression of idols, so also the true God makes images of Himself to multiply the worship of Himself. Men and women are designed by God to make His character visible, living in a way that tells the truth about God to the rest of creation.

That is mankind's identity: we are to be conduits for the worship of God. We live contrary to our identity, design, and purpose, when we pursue the self-actualization of our basest fleshly desires. Genuine, abundant life is not found in the pursuit of our own lordship. It is found in humble submission to the Lord of glory, walking in the way of His commandments, and trusting Him to show us what it means to be truly human in this life.

6 John MacArthur and Richard Mayhue, eds., *Biblical Doctrine: A Systematic Summary of Bible Truth* (Wheaton: Crossway, 2017), 410.

Fallen Masterpiece

In an interview with the BBC, Martyn Lloyd-Jones captured the internally inconsistent view of human identity that plagues our society. He said, "The contemporary conception of man, on the one hand, doesn't make enough of man, and, on the other, makes too much of him."[7]

It's true. We don't make enough of man, because we consider man to be a mere animal, not really distinct from the other creatures, not an image bearer of Almighty God. Prevailing views on abortion and euthanasia signal that when a person is deemed to be not useful or too much of an inconvenience, he can be discarded.

On the other hand, we make too much of man. We flatter ourselves into suggesting that man is basically good—a morally upright being, who just needs to live out his authentic inner self. Semi-catechetical phrases of the secular religion include reassurances that "You're amazing, just the way you are," and "No one can judge you." We're counseled, "Find your truth and live your truth," which basically means, "Fabricate your own version of reality, and insist on it!" These presuppositions lead people to believe that they can create male and female in their own image, determine when a baby becomes a person, and can define marriage however they please.

This demonstrates that even when man makes too much of himself, he winds up not making enough of himself. The embrace of transgenderism leads men and women to treat themselves like Frankenstein-like experiments, often ending in irreversible self-mutilation and sterilization. The embrace of abortion turns parents into murderers of their own defenseless children. The embrace of homosexuality leads to the denigration and trivialization of the most solemn of human relationships. In seeking to exalt himself, man ruins himself.

Instead of that schizophrenic view of man, Scripture identifies man as the image of God. Joel Beeke makes the comment that man is "a fallen masterpiece of God." I think that really captures it well. Man is a masterpiece. We are masterpieces because we are made in the image of God and therefore we have inherent dignity. Our lives are worth being protected because we are the closest reflection of the life and character of our Creator.

But man is a *fallen* masterpiece. We have not remained in that "very good" (Gen. 1:31) state in which God created us. We haven't lost the image of God (James 3:9), but we have marred it (Col. 3:10). Something has

7 "Joan Bakewell Interviews Dr. Martyn Lloyd Jones," https://www.youtube.com/watch?v=-vbydx95tVQ (accessed December 2023).

gone terribly wrong with us, so the altogether optimistic views of man and his moral goodness are a wild caricature of reality. Men and women are lost, bound for hell, and totally beholden to the sovereign grace of God for any remedy to our hopeless predicament.

There is a glory and dignity in the human race, but this is derived from the glory and dignity of God, whose image man is. God multiplies and magnifies His own glory by creating images of Himself—pictures of His beauty, glory, and righteousness—in the crown and apex of His creation.

REFLECT THE CHARACTER OF THE ONE WHOSE IMAGE YOU BEAR

To be created in God's image, then, is to belong to God, to be responsible to obey His law, and thereby to reflect His glory and thereby tell the truth about His character to the rest of creation. The God in whose image man is made will be the God before whom he must stand for judgment.

This means that men and women are not free to order their lives however they see fit. You are not free to forge your own identity. You are what God says you are, and you must order your life as your Creator commands. You may not rebel against God's created order by identifying as a different gender, because He has made you male or female in His image. God has designed to receive glory from His creatures as the males or females He has created them to be.

If you are a woman, you cannot glorify God by attempting to live as a man. If you are a man, you cannot glorify God by attempting to live as a woman. God has designed to receive particular praise from your life as the man or woman He created you to be.

Similarly, you may not rebel against the created order of God by pursuing romantic and sexual relationships with members of the same sex. He created men and women to complement one another—to image forth the unity and diversity of the Godhead.

Just as there is unity of essence and diversity of persons in the Trinity, so also is there to be a unity of humanity and diversity of gender in the marriage relationship. Homosexual "marriage" distorts the picture of God that mankind is designed to be.

Bearing the image of Another obligates you to the One whose image you bear.

"Whose image is on this coin?" Jesus asked.

"Caesar's," replied His disciples. And Jesus said, "Then, render to Caesar the things that are Caesar's" (Matt. 22:20–21). But whose image is upon this man or upon this woman? Scripture tells us the answer: "God's image." Jesus' reply is applicable: "Then render . . . to God the things that are God's" (Matt. 22:21).

You are accountable to the One in whose image you have been created, and therefore you must render your life to Him.

Study Questions:

1. What are some examples of how you have seen the culture define human identity by their desires? How do the truths in this chapter help you offer a response?
2. In what way is self-identification a direct affront to God's own name?
3. How are attacks on young earth creationism connected with sexual rebellion?
4. What are the key implications of man being an image bearer of God?
5. In what ways does being an image bearer give humans a dignity above all other creatures? How does our culture live inconsistently with that?
6. Explain what Martyn Lloyd-Jones meant when he said, "The contemporary conception of man, on the one hand, doesn't make enough of man, and, on the other, makes too much of him."
7. Explain in your own words why and how being an image bearer makes a person accountable to God.

2

Gender Confusion

The World's Suicidal Infatuation with Self-Creation

THE PREVIOUS CHAPTER showed us the foundational markers of human identity. First of all, man is a creature: "God created man" (Gen. 1:27). We are not God; we are creatures of the one true and living God. As a result, we are accountable to our Creator, we are subject to the identity He has given us, and we are subject to Him as the Ruler of our lives.

Second, man is the image of God: "God created man in His own image, in the image of God He created him" (Gen. 1:27). Mankind is designed by God to make His character visible, living in a way that tells the truth about God to the rest of creation.

As image-bearers, then, we humans are not free to forge our own identities; we *receive* our identity from the One whose image we bear. Our identity is derived not from our own sense of self, but from God's revelation of whom He has made us to be.

A third foundational marker of our identity as human beings: man is gendered: "God created man in His own image, in the image of God He created him; male and female He created them." We are not only creatures and image-bearers; we bear God's image together in the beautiful distinctiveness of being male or female. Our gender is thus deeply connected to our identity as image-bearing creatures. It is part of who God says we are, and it relates fundamentally to how each image-bearer will glorify God by representing Him to the world.

We really cannot miss this. Gender—and, in particular, the gender binary—is fundamental to the biblical doctrine of mankind. What it means to be an image-bearer is to be either male or female. Therefore, any attempt to change male into female, and certainly any attempt to find a space in between male and female, is a fundamental attack both on the authority of God and on one's own humanity.

Transgender ideology is just such an attack. It is a suicidal attempt to replace God as the Creator and determiner of identity, a species of self-exaltation that aims at self-creation. Transgenderism is the creature's attempt to escape from the accountability of being a creature, which is equivalent to an attempt to uncreate oneself. It is the proud, rebellious protest: "I will create male and female in my image!" Or, in some cases: "I will be neither male nor female, and therefore I will undermine my very humanity itself!"

THE TRANSGENDER DELUSION

The chaos of that worldview is wreaking havoc all over our culture. It seems transgenderism is the peak of the absurdity that must be embraced after denying the existence of truth altogether.[1] There is no more brazen denial of reality than to suggest that a man can be a woman if he feels like it.

Thirty years ago, everyone regarded the concept of a pregnant man as a comedic fantasy. Danny DeVito and Arnold Schwarzenegger starred in the 1994 movie, *Junior,* in which Schwarzenegger's character, a male, became pregnant. No one was tempted to take that any more seriously than stories of Santa Claus or the Easter Bunny. But just three decades later, the propagandists shout, "Trans men *are* men!" That is, women pretending to be men are claimed to be "real men" (whatever that means), and, of course, because some of these women can still get pregnant, the regime demands that you confess that men can get pregnant. If you don't, you're a transphobic bigot who should be banished from polite society.

In fact, this delusion seems to have no ceiling. When the newest Supreme Court Justice, Ketanji Brown-Jackson, was interviewed by Congress, she was asked to define the word "woman." She said she couldn't give such a definition because she wasn't a biologist.[2] That is nothing but the consistent application of a worldview that denies the existence of absolute truth.

---

1 Portions of this section are adapted from Michael Riccardi, "What is Truth? Reason, Relativism, and Reality," in *Right Thinking for a Culture in Chaos*, eds. John MacArthur and Nathan Busenitz (Eugene, OR: Harvest House Publishers, 2023), 41–55. Used by Permission.

2 Mark Moore and Samuel Chamberlain, "Judge Jackson declines to define 'woman,' says she's 'not a biologist,'" *New York Post,* March 23, 2022, https://nypost.com/2022/03/23/sen-blackburn-slams-judge-jackson-on-definition-of-woman (accessed December 2023).

Downstream from that denial of reality, one grants oneself permission to alter the canons of basic biology to fit preconceived social policy.

In the recent documentary, *What is a Woman?*, conservative commentator Matt Walsh interviewed several people who embraced transgender ideology, seeking to answer that very question: If anyone can be a woman if he or she feels like it, what precisely is a woman?

He never received a satisfactory answer. In fact, during one interview with a gender studies professor, Walsh said he wanted to "get to the truth."

The professor replied, "I'm really uncomfortable with that language. . . . It sounds deeply transphobic to me." The professor eventually threatened to stop the interview, saying, "You keep invoking the word 'truth,' which is condescending and rude."[3]

Those desiring to embrace absurdity and to deny reality recognize that truth is the enemy of their worldview. But it's not that truth is transphobic; truth is not afraid of those with gender dysphoria. In reality, "trans" is truth-phobic. The transgender worldview recognizes that it's grounded in subjectivist fantasy, and it fears the light of truth will expose its irrationality.

It's important to say: Everyone knows that transgenderism is a charade. The emperor has no clothes. Christian or not, no one really believes that a man actually can become a woman. But it's as if everyone is agreeing to play pretend. And it's such a curious delusion that it's worth asking why such a social contract exists. It's not as if transgender people are a large constituency; the entire LGBTQ movement comprises only about seven percent of the U.S. population. Why do people pretend what they know to be true is false? And why do they insist that everyone else play along?

The answer is twofold. First, people go along with the transgender charade because they know if they don't, they'll be ridiculed, accosted, and canceled. Our society tolerates the utterly absurd in order to not be subjected to a kind of ostracism that could leave them bankrupt and alone.

But more importantly, if people pretend there's no standard by which transgenderism is wrong, they can pretend there's no standard by which *their* sin is wrong. If men can be women, truth can be false, and morality can be entirely upended. In other words, if there is an absolute standard of truth, then everyone is accountable to the God of truth, whose law condemns them for their own sins. And that they simply cannot tolerate. "Sure! Lies can be truth! Men can be women! Anything you say, as long as I can

---

3 Matt Walsh, *What Is a Woman?* https://www.dailywire.com/videos/what-is-a-woman (accessed December 2023).

sin in peace!" They "suppress the truth in unrighteousness" (Rom. 1:18), denying the very existence of truth itself, to make provision for their flesh, in regard to its lusts (Rom. 13:14).

To put it in the words of Jesus,

> This is the judgment, that the Light has come into the world, and men loved the darkness rather than the Light, for their deeds were evil. For everyone who does evil hates the Light, and does not come to the Light for fear that his deeds will be exposed. But he who practices the truth comes to the Light, so that his deeds may be manifested as having been wrought in God. (John 3:19–21)

People reject the truth—they reject what is true and the standard of truth itself—not because it is intellectually honest (it's not), but because to embrace it would require them to expose themselves as sinners who are accountable to God's standard of judgment.

PATRIARCHY IN HEELS

The transgender delusion started in the public discourse in earnest not long after the Obergefell decision that legalized so-called homosexual "marriage." In 2015, *Glamour* magazine gave their Woman of the Year Award to none other than Bruce Jenner, who began calling himself "Caitlyn." The Woman of the Year Award went to someone who wasn't a woman at all.

Richard Levine, a man who dresses as a woman and calls himself Rachel, was appointed by President Biden to be the U.S. Assistant Secretary of Health for the Department of Health and Human Services. He is celebrated as the first female four-star admiral in the U.S. Public Health Service Commissioned Corps. But of course, he's not female at all. As a result of those spurious honors, USA Today named Levine one of their "women of the year" for 2022.

William Thomas was a three-year swimmer on the men's team at the University of Pennsylvania. He was ranked #462 in the world in men's NCAA swimming competition. Before the 2021–2022 season, William said he identified as a woman and called himself "Lia." He joined the women's swim team at Penn, and he won the NCAA Championship in the 500-meter freestyle, besting the young women he was competing against by more than a full second. He finished college ranking #1 in the world in NCAA women's swimming.

Boyd Burton is a mixed martial arts fighter who says he identifies as a woman and calls himself Fallon Fox. In a 2014 competition, he fractured the skull of the actual woman he was fighting against. One wonders why any woman would agree to compete in a mixed martial arts bout with someone who is physiologically male. It's one thing to pretend and to be politically correct when it doesn't cost a fractured skull. But given the foreseeability of that kind of danger, why would any intelligent woman go through with it?

And it seems the answer is the same for why any female athlete goes through with competing against a biologically male opponent: the fear of being called a transphobe and a bigot—the fear of being canceled and shamed into oblivion for refusing to play pretend. It used to be that pressuring a woman to subject herself to being battered by a mentally ill man was called abuse. Now, apparently, it's called feminism.

That's what's most stupefying. This whole charade is performed in the name of liberating women from oppression, but I doubt that people could design a system more oppressive to women than this. Men are allowed into women's sports, and those women are placed at an unfair competitive disadvantage. Men are allowed into women's locker rooms and bathrooms, and their privacy is invaded. Men are allowed into women's prisons, and criminally minded men prey on women who have no way to protect themselves. It truly is ludicrous social policy.

For all the talk about wanting to "smash the patriarchy," the woman of the year is a man; the purported best female college swimmer in the country is a man; the best female MMA fighter is a man; the first female four-star admiral in the Public Health Service is a man; the greatest female *Jeopardy* champion is a man. What message are these feminists sending? That men are better than women—even at being women? It seems like transgenderism ensures that the patriarchy always wins in the end. In fact, that observation has led one social commentator to say: "Hard truth: the trans movement *is* the patriarchy. Just in makeup and heels."

THE DEATH CULT

That all may sound rhetorical and theoretical. But it's not just faceless structures and systems of society that suffer. Consequences exist for real people.

Transgender ideology is the perverted, creedal confession of a death-cult, whose high priesthood has infiltrated pop-culture, mainstream media, and the educational system. They mercilessly destroy the lives of the victims they're able to woo into their coven.

Precious people willingly mutilate themselves in search of a quasi-salvation that never comes. You see the forearms of young women, whose muscle tissues have been harvested in order to create fake, non-functioning male parts, and it's enough to make you weep. And that's only a fraction of the literal carnage that could be described.

As a teenager, Cari sought to "transition" to being male by taking testosterone and having a double mastectomy. A few years later, she recognized the mistake she had made and decided to *de*transition—to stop taking testosterone and begin living as a woman again. She writes of the effects of her choices: "I'm a real live 22-year-old woman with a scarred chest and a broken voice and a 5 o'clock shadow because I couldn't face the idea of growing up to be a woman."[4] She goes on to lament the likelihood that she'll never be able to have children.

Another detransitioner who calls herself "Crash" writes,

> There is a very deep, painful symbolism behind losing your original voice and having no way of getting it back. For many of us it is not the physical changes themselves that are troubling, but what they represent. . . . they remind me of what I did to myself, how I rejected and betrayed myself, how deeply I took other people's hatred into my own body. My body is now marked forever by that hatred and that can be a lot to carry. Many of us have struggled with feeling like we have ruined ourselves.[5]

Precious people, made in the image of God, are the collateral damage of the transgender death cult.

Such are the consequences of the denial of the existence of objective truth, the rejection of God, and the rejection of humans' creation in the image of God. In the name of expressing himself, man destroys himself. In the name of being true to his "authentic self," he ruins himself.

An Anti-Biblical Worldview

Why does our culture tolerate such manifest absurdity that has such horrifying consequences? We've already looked at several suggested reasons, but it is partly owing to how seamlessly transgenderism fits with the secular worldview of our times—a worldview that Carl Trueman calls "expressive individualism."[6]

---

4 Ryan T. Anderson, *When Harry Became Sally: Responding to the Transgender Movement* (New York: Encounter Books, 2019), 56.

5 Anderson, *When Harry Became Sally*, 74–75.

6 Carl R. Trueman, *The Rise and Triumph of the Modern Self: Cultural Amnesia, Expressive Individualism, and the Road to Sexual Revolution* (Wheaton: Crossway, 2020), 46.

Expressive Individualism

Expressive individualism is the idea that "each of us finds our meaning by giving expression to our own feelings and desires."[7] The Enlightenment philosopher Rene Descartes is famous for the dictum, "I think; therefore I am." Expressive individualism is captured by the motto, "I feel, therefore I am." Such a worldview reasons, "I am what I feel I am. And in order for me to be my authentic self, I must give expression to that feeling. Any contradiction of my psychological beliefs about myself—even something as non-aggressive as someone refusing to affirm those feelings—disturbs my sense of inner well-being. Because I *am* my feelings, your lack of affirmation is a threat to my very identity. It is violence against my personhood."

That captures western culture of the last fifteen years. This is why words are so often spoken of as being "weaponized": everything is a weapon if someone is under attack when his or her feelings aren't affirmed. This is why people need "trigger warnings" and "safe spaces," places where people can avoid anything they might not like to hear—from "micro-aggressions" all the way to "hate speech."

Transgenderism coheres perfectly with this culture of expressive individualism. If my feelings *are* my identity, and any contradiction of those feelings is a threat to my very personhood, then the facts of my name, the pronouns I use, and even the physiology of my body itself must be changed to suit my inner sense of self.

If you don't affirm me in making those changes, you hate me. You don't just disagree with a choice I make; these feelings are me. Any lack of wholehearted affirmation is the same as wanting me to die. This is nothing more than expressive individualism applied to my gender expression.

A homosexual activist group, that calls itself "The Human Rights Campaign" defines gender as "one's innermost concept of self as male, female, a blend of both, or neither—how individuals perceive themselves and what they call themselves."[8] Nancy Pearcey characterizes this attitude helpfully: "We do not discover our gender identity, as though it were an objective fact. Instead we declare our identity. We speak ourselves into existence."[9] She's exactly right. We declare ourselves to be in the place of God, creating male

---

7 Trueman, 46.

8 Nancy Pearcey, *Love Thy Body: Answering Hard Questions about Life and Sexuality* (Grand Rapids: Baker, 2018), 214.

9 Pearcey, *Love Thy Body*, 215.

and female in our image. Self-creation is the absurd delusion of the expressive individualism that undergirds transgender ideology.

Gnosticism

Transgender ideology also shares a fundamental affinity with the old heresy of gnosticism, the second-century Greek philosophical school that taught that the spiritual is inherently good and the material is inherently evil.

The Greek phrase *sōma sēma* (the body is a tomb) was a popular gnostic motto. They saw the body as a prison that incarcerated the true self of the spirit, and they longed for death when the spirit could be liberated from its material prison.

Transgenderism is a species of that kind of thinking. The fundamental premise of transgender ideology is that our real self is found within us. Again, "I am what I feel I am, on the inside." The external, material reality of the body is only accidental to the real person. In fact, in a BBC documentary on transgenderism and children, a trans activist is quoted as saying, "It doesn't matter what living meat skeleton you've been born in; it's what you feel that defines you."[10] My authentic self is whatever matches my internal feelings. The physical body is just a meat skeleton that my inner-self possesses as an instrument. My body is not me, in any meaningful sense.

Therefore, if my physical body imprisons my immaterial authentic self, I should be free to alter my body—even through crippling hormones and mutilating surgeries—in order to make my body match my feelings. If a conflict exists between the body and the mind, transgender ideology says the mind always wins. One commentator has observed that the foundational ontological assumption undergirding transgender ideology is a low view of the body. And as we'll see in the next chapter, that is antithetical to the biblical worldview, which has an exceptionally high view of the spiritual *and* the physical, of the soul *and* the body.

Inherently Contradictory

Besides this, the transgender worldview is inherently contradictory and internally incoherent. As much as transgenderism assumes a low view of the body, it places an awful lot of importance upon the body. On the one hand, the body is so lowly regarded "that the real self is fundamentally separate from

10 As cited in Pearcey, *Love Thy Body*, 197.

the material body."[11] On the other, the body is so important to gender identity that it must be subjected to radical, invasive, expensive, and dangerous hormone treatments and surgeries to be conformed to the inner sense of self.

Trueman put it this way: the body "is both irrelevant to identity such that it is no ultimate guide to who we are and it is also vital to identity in that it may, if desired, be modified to fit the inner sense."[12] More than that, people claim that the body is so vital that if taxpayers don't pay for gender-reassignment surgeries, transgender people will experience such dissonance that they will commit suicide.

Another contradiction is the claim that gender is an artificial social construct that can be totally fluid, but then those who purport this rely on rigid stereotypes to say people can be trapped in the wrong body. If a girl likes to play with guns and trucks, it's a sign that she may really be a boy. But if gender is so fluid that it can't be indicated by chromosomes, DNA, and anatomy, how can it be so rigid as to be predicted by shared hobbies and interests?

On the one hand, we're told that there is no such thing as a boy; gender is just a fluid spectrum. On the other hand, we're told that if a female child likes guns, trucks, and sports, she must really be boy on the inside.

A third contradiction concerns the supposed subjectivism of morality alongside the rigid dogmatism of their worldview. On the one hand, expressive individualism issues in a radical subjectivism; people must be free to do whatever they want according to their deeply held beliefs and feelings. On the other hand, if someone refuses to use another's preferred pronouns or gender-denying name, he must be canceled. If you don't confess with your mouth that "Trans women *are* women," and believe in your heart that "Men can be 'birthing persons' too," you're a bigot who should lose your job and be banished from polite company. Everyone is free to be whomever they wish—as long as they don't disagree with me.

WHERE DO WE GO FROM HERE?

What is our response to the madness? It can only be to declare the Word of God to all those who rebel against it. The only response to the deception and the lies of the culture is to proclaim the truth. And for the truth, we must turn to the God of truth, who has spoken to us in the Word of truth—the inspired, inerrant, and infallible Word of God—the Bible.

---

11 Anderson, *When Harry Became Sally*, 3.

12 Trueman, *The Rise and Triumph of the Modern Self*, 369.

In the next chapter, we will explore five biblical truths about gender that we must learn and live by, so that we would live in faithful obedience to the Lordship of Jesus in the midst of the corruption of the world we are called to serve.

Study Questions:

1. Explain in your own words the relationship between (a) mankind as God's image bearer and (b) mankind as being male or female.
2. In light of the above, what is the significance of living out of accord with one's biological gender, especially as it relates to the Lordship of God?
3. How would you respond if a friend or co-worker told you he or she couldn't define what a woman was?
4. Why do you think the professor mentioned in the chapter believed the concept of "the truth" was transphobic?
5. Given that transgender people make up such a small constituency of the United States, why do you think transgender ideology enjoys such widespread cultural support?
6. Explain what passages like John 3:19–21 and Romans 1:18 have to do with this discussion.
7. What stands out to you about the testimonies of detransitioners like Cari and Crash?
8. In what ways have you seen the worldview of "expressive individualism" exert influence on the thinking of those around you? Can you identify any areas where it's exerted influence on your own thinking? If so, how should you respond?
9. In what ways does transgender ideology have a contradictory view of the body?

3

Male and Female He Created Them

A Biblical Doctrine of Gender

As MENTIONED, GENESIS 1:27 defines human identity in three fundamental ways: We are creatures, we are image bearers, and we are gendered. "God created man in His own image, in the image of God He created him; male and female He created them."

God's human creatures magnify their Creator by bearing His image in unity through the distinctiveness of being male or female. Gender, therefore, is foundational both to our identity and to the specific ways we bring glory to God as we represent Him to the world.

If the last chapter diagnosed our culture's sickness concerning gender ideology, this chapter serves as the remedy that treats the disease. We will consider five scriptural truths that will yield for us the biblical doctrine of gender. These truths will equip us to speak God's Word boldly and compassionately to a culture that desperately needs it.

Granted by Our Creator

The first truth is that gender is granted, or bestowed, by our Creator. That comes, once again, from Genesis 1:27: "Male and female He created them." We are creatures, not gods. Our duty is to represent Him, not express ourselves apart from Him. And God has created us to represent Him as distinctively male or female.

This is radically opposed to the transgender ideology, which claims gender is a social construct, spoken into existence by the sovereignty of each individual. This text teaches us that we are not self-creators. We do not self-identify—as anything. We are not free to forge our own identity. We *receive* our identity from a God who identifies us according to His sovereign prerogative—a prerogative

He exercises as our Creator (Acts 17:24; Ps. 24:1). Since He is Creator, He is "Lord of heaven and earth" (Acts 17:24; Ps. 115:3), and therefore He is the One who "gives to all people life and breath and all things" (Acts 17:25). That is, all things are bestowed upon us by our Creator and Lord.

Therefore, as long as you did not self-create, you are not free to self-identify. You are what God says you are, and you must conduct yourself in the way God says you must. You may not rebel against the created order of God by identifying as a different gender. Only One gets to say, "I am who I am," and that is the self-existent Triune Creator, the One who really did speak the world into existence—the only One who says, "Let there be," and it is so.

In First Corinthians 6, Paul told believers that, since Christ had purchased them by His own blood, they were not their own but belonged to Him: "Do you not know . . . that you are not your own? For you have been bought with a price" (6:19–20). The conclusion he drew from this was, "Therefore glorify God *in your body*" (6:20).

Christians are God's people by redemption, and that creates ethical obligations for our conduct. Well, though not all human beings are God's people by redemption, they are God's possession by creation (Acts 17:24). In that sense, Paul's exhortation may be given to all people without exception. Because you didn't create yourself, you aren't lord of yourself.

Since all of God's image bearers are His possession, He has the prerogative to declare to everyone, "You are not your own. Therefore, glorify God in your body." There is a very real sense in which your Creator points to your body and says, "*My* body, *My* choice."

Gender is not determined by feelings, self-perceptions, or preferences of the creature. Gender is granted by the sovereign prerogative of our Creator.

GROUNDED IN BIOLOGY

Related to that, gender is grounded in biology. We see that by observing that God made the gender binary: God created mankind male and female, one or the other. The text does not say, "In the image of God He created him, male, and female, and agender, and genderqueer, and genderfluid, and pangender, and two-spirit He created them." No, God's design from the beginning is that mankind is either male or female.

Further, the God who created mankind male and female called the male "Adam" (Gen. 2:20) and "the man" (Gen. 2:8, 15, 16, 18–25), and then He formed the female, Eve (Gen. 3:20), out of Adam's body (Gen. 2:19, 22), and Adam named her "woman" (Gen. 2:23). Thus, manhood is inextricably linked to maleness, and womanhood is inextricably linked to femaleness. Gender is inextricably rooted in our biology.

Still further, from the beginning, "woman" is described as an *ezer kenegdō*, a helper suitable to Adam (Gen. 2:18). The Hebrew term *néged* means that the woman was corresponding to, or complementary to, the man. She was sufficiently like the man that she was suitable for him in a way none of the animals were. She was human, just as he was. But she was not identical to him. There was correspondence but not identity. There was likeness but not sameness. There was unity, but there was also diversity.

The specific task for which the woman is a suitable help to the man is the fulfillment of the creation mandate. Immediately after we're told that God created His image bearers male and female, we read of God's charge to mankind: "God blessed them; and God said to them, 'Be fruitful and multiply, and fill the earth'" (Gen. 1:28).

God created man male and female and commanded them to reproduce—to create more people like themselves. God brings all the animals of creation to Adam, and none of them is a helper suitable to aid Adam in the fulfillment of this divine mandate. The only creature suitable for man is woman, because only the union between man and woman—alike in their humanity, but distinct in their gender—can result in the fruitfulness that God had commanded of them.

This means that the complementarity of man's and woman's bodies are essential to their identity as man and woman. Gender is fundamentally grounded in biology, because maleness and femaleness are designed by God with an eye to reproduction. And in that task of fruitful multiplication, the man's and the woman's bodies are perfectly suited to their distinctive roles. The man gives, and the woman receives. The man provides the seed, and the woman nurtures that life in her womb until it's time to give birth, at which time she continues to nurture that life by giving nutrients from her own body in feeding. What it means to be woman is to be one whose body—in principle—can suitably help a man to walk in obedience to God's command to multiply and fill the earth.

The moment we're told God made humans male and female, we read of God's command to be fruitful and multiply. The moment the woman is discovered to be the suitable helper for the man in the way the animals are not, we read, "For this reason a man shall leave his father and his mother, and be joined to his wife; and they shall become one flesh" (Gen. 2:24).

Mention of male and female is immediately followed by a reference to procreation. A reference to the man and woman immediately issues in marriage and the one-flesh union through which procreation takes place. Definitional to manhood and womanhood—to maleness and femaleness—is the sexual complementarity that issues in childbearing. Gender, therefore, is inextricably grounded in biology and is irrevocably and immutably binary. This is God's very good design from the beginning (Gen. 1:31).

So much is gender grounded in biology that same terms for "man" and "woman" (*ish* and *isshah*) and "male" and "female" (*zākār* and *neqēvah*) are used of animals. As Noah prepared them to board the ark ahead of the flood, God commanded, "And of every living thing of all flesh, you shall bring two of every kind into the ark, to keep them alive with you; they shall be male and female" (Gen. 6:19). For the animals' existence to be preserved, Noah had to bring both male and female into the ark, so that, after the flood passed, they could reproduce after their kind. This means that essential to maleness and femaleness are those biological functions which, in principle (barring any physiological dysfunction), allow for reproduction.

Therefore, gender is not a social construct grounded in the mind of the creature. Since the same terms are used of animals as well as humans, and since animals don't have gender identity distinct from their biology, "gender has a biological component firmly rooted in the physical body."[1]

According to Scripture, God has designed each person's gender to correspond with his or her biological sex.[2] God could have made more than two genders, but He didn't. Something about this gender binary in His creatures reflects the glory of His good design (Gen. 1:31), and it is woven throughout all human relationships: man and woman, boy and girl, husband and wife, father and mother, son and daughter, brother and sister, king and queen, prince and princess, and so on.

Not only this, but Jesus Himself affirmed the gender binary. So often people claim that Jesus never said anything about LGBTQ issues, but that's not so. When the Pharisees tested Jesus with questions about marriage and divorce, He answered by saying, "Have you not read that He who created them from the beginning 'made them male and female,' and said, 'For this reason a man shall leave his father and mother and be joined to his wife, and the two shall become one flesh'?" (Matt. 19:4–5).

---

1 Beeke and Smalley, *Reformed Systematic Theology*, 2:210.

2 Beeke and Smalley, *Reformed Systematic Theology*, 2:210.

Jesus effectively said, "This is the way God has done marriage from the beginning. It is His design, and it is the foundation of all humanity." He affirmed that all human civilization is grounded in this binary of the biological sexes: male and female, for the purpose of one-flesh union with a view to having children.

But what about people who can't have children? If manhood and womanhood are so geared toward reproduction, are infertile couples less men or women because of their infertility? No, because, while being gives rise to function, being is not grounded in function. What something is doesn't depend exclusively on what it does.

Because of the curse of sin, dysfunction is in the creation (Gen. 3:17; 5:29), but that dysfunction does not destroy God's creation or overturn His design. Just because things don't always work the way they were designed to work, it doesn't mean that the norm isn't normal, or that nature isn't natural.

A similar response can be given to the oft-raised objection of intersex people. How can we say there is an immutable gender binary when we know there are people with genetic or physical anomalies that result in both male and female genitalia or dysfunctional reproductive organs?

Those with disorders of sexual development do not constitute a third gender. Some people who are born without two functioning legs, but it's still right to say that God made human beings as bipedal creatures. Physical anomalies are the exceptions that prove the rule. In the same way, it's still right to say, "God made human beings as males or females." The existence of biological anomalies are the exceptions that prove the rule.[3]

A Gift of God's Loving Care

A third truth about gender that we glean from the Scriptures is that it is a gift of God's loving care. In Psalm 139, after David praised God for His omniscience and omnipresence, he praised God for His intricate craftsmanship in knitting David together, even in his mother's womb:

> For You formed my inward parts; You wove me in my mother's womb. I will give thanks to You, for I am fearfully and wonderfully made; Wonderful are Your works, And my soul knows it very well. My frame was not hidden from You, When I was made in secret, And skillfully wrought in the depths of the earth. (Ps. 139:13–15)

3 For good measure, those who have disorders of sexual development need to be loved, accepted, and cared for—not used as political pawns to justify perversion.

This passage emphasizes how intentionally, carefully, and purposefully God Himself fashions each image-bearer in his or her mother's womb. He is like a master artisan, skillfully weaving the body of the unborn child together to function as a cohesive whole (Job 10:11). Each one of us is skillfully wrought by the wisdom of the God who knows every thought we think and every word we speak (Ps. 139:4). Each one is fearfully and wonderfully made with the care of the loving God, who hems us in behind and before and leads us by His right hand (Ps. 139:5). He handcrafts our bodies as we grow in our mothers' wombs. It is unthinkable that a God who is so wise, skillful, and loving could fashion the wrong body for the wrong soul—even in one instance.

That means that our gendered bodies are the gifts of God's loving care, through which He graciously reveals to us this vital aspect of our identity. Our bodies are God's kind revelation of our gender. Our gender isn't declared *by* us; it is revealed *to* us in the body that was skillfully wrought and wonderfully made by our loving Creator.

And if our God has fashioned each of us so carefully and purposefully, our response must be to receive that identity as a gift from Him, not to argue with Him about it, and thereby call into question His wisdom or His goodness. Isaiah 45:9 says, "Woe to the one who quarrels with his Maker— An earthenware vessel among the vessels of earth! Will the clay say to the potter, 'What are you doing?' Or the thing you are making say, 'He has no hands'?" Paul asks, similarly, "Who are you, O man, who answers back to God? The thing molded will not say to the molder, 'Why did you make me like this,' will it?" (Rom. 9:20).

It would be absurd for clay to dispute with the potter about being made the wrong way. That would mean the clay would be exalting itself outside of the bounds of its proper domain. In the same way, it would be absurd for the creature to dispute with the Creator about being made in the wrong body. That one would be exalting himself outside the bounds of his proper domain, intruding into the throne room of the Sovereign God.

Acts 17:26 tells us that God determines the time and place of our birth. He determines our ethnic background and the families into which we are born. He even determines our physical features. We don't choose any of these things. We look around at the country and state and city we were born in, we look at the color of our skin, we even look in the mirror, and we conclude, "God has made me like this. This is who I am." The proper response to God for all those things is to give Him thanks (Ps. 139:14) as the Giver of all good things (James 1:17).[4] The same must be true when it comes to our bodies.

Ultimately, this boils down to a question of authority, knowledge, and trustworthiness. "Who has the right to tell me what to do? Who knows what is best for me to do? Who loves me and wants what is best for me?"[5]

Because God is our Creator and we are His image bearers, He has the authority, and we do not. Because God is all wise and perfect in wisdom, He knows what is best, and we must confess our ignorance and finitude. And because God is compassionate and gracious and abounding in lovingkindness (Exod. 34:6), we can trust Him to want what is best for us, even more than we can trust ourselves, we whose hearts are deceitful and desperately wicked (Jer. 17:9).

The Goodness of the Body

A fourth truth about gender that Scripture reveals is that the body is a good thing. As mentioned in the previous chapter, the fundamental premise of transgender ideology is that our real self is found within us.

This ideology teaches that the external, material reality of my body is only accidental to the real me. My body is not me; my identity—my authentic self—is my internal feelings. I happen to possess a body that can be wielded as the instrument of my internal self, but if the body is an impediment to the expression of what's inside, then I should feel perfectly free to alter my body to make it match my feelings.

An Ordered and Purposeful Creation

This low view of the body originates in pagan denials of the biblical doctrines of nature and creation. That's true not only of second-century Gnosticism, but also of nineteenth-century Darwinism.

The creationist understanding of nature is teleological: The creation is ordered and reflects the Creator's purpose. "The heavens declare the glory of God, and the sky above proclaims his handiwork" (Ps. 19:1, ESV). God's "invisible attributes, His eternal power and divine nature, have been clearly

4 "Identity Crisis: Biblical Clarity for a Culture Characterized by Gender Confusion," in *Right Thinking for a Culture in Chaos*, eds. John MacArthur and Nathan Busenitz (Eugene, OR: Harvest House, 2023), 111.

5 Andrew T. Walker, *God and the Transgender Debate: What Does the Bible Actually Say About Gender Identity?* (Charlotte, NC: The Good Book Company, 2017), 39.

seen, being understood through what has been made" (Rom. 1:20). The creation embodies meaningful order and reveals truth about God to man.

But Darwin's rejection of the Creator and His creation in favor of evolutionary theory led to viewing the creation as purposeless and random. As a result, the natural world can no longer be trusted to reliably reveal the character and will of God to His creatures. Nancy Pearcey explains the consequences of that line of thinking:

> The next step in the logic is crucial: If nature does not reveal God's will, then it is a morally neutral realm where humans may impose their will. There is nothing in nature that humans are morally obligated to respect. Nature becomes the realm of value-neutral facts, available to serve whatever values humans may choose. And because the human body is part of nature, it too is demoted to the level of an amoral mechanism, subject to the will of the autonomous self. If the body has no intrinsic purpose, built in by God, then all that matters are human purposes. The body is reduced to a clump of matter—a collection of atoms and molecules, not essentially different from any other chance configuration of matter. It is raw material to be manipulated and controlled to serve the human agenda, like any other natural resource.[6]

The atheistic view of nature leads to the dichotomizing of the body and the soul, a dichotomizing of the body and the person. The body is demeaned as that which is extrinsic or accidental to the person, rather than an essential component of the person and a key piece of our identity.

Then, when it comes to our gender and sexual orientation, if our sexuality is not derived from the objective testimony of the body—which, as an aspect of a meaningful, purposeful, ordered cosmos, is a reliable revelation of ourselves from God to us—then it will become something we impose on the body.[7] Transgenderism is the result of such a pagan cosmology.

Psychosomatic Unity

The biblical worldview stands in stark contrast to this view of the body. Nature is purposeful and is ordered by God, and the body is a part of nature that reveals God's purposes.

Christianity has an exceptionally high view of the spiritual *and* the physical, of the soul *and* the body. It regards a human as the complex, integrated unity of body and soul.

6 Pearcey, *Love Thy Body*, 24.

7 Pearcey, *Love Thy Body*, 31.

God created the first man and the first woman as body-soul entities. They had a physical, embodied existence on the sixth day of creation, before the curse brought on by sin, and God pronounced these first people to be, "very good" (Gen. 1:31). Humanity was at its purest in Eden, and the man and the woman were both *embodied* souls.

And the rest of Scripture underscores that "very good" view of the material body. For example, First Corinthians 7:34 speaks of holiness "both in body and spirit," using a term for both the material and immaterial aspects of man to refer to the whole person. Second Corinthians 7:1 is similar: "Let us cleanse ourselves from all defilement of flesh and spirit, perfecting holiness in the fear of God." In Psalm 63:1, David said, "O God, You are my God; I shall seek You earnestly; / My soul thirsts for You, my flesh yearns for You, / In a dry and weary land where there is no water." Both soul and flesh—material and immaterial aspects of man—long for communion with God. Beeke and Smalley conclude, "We must view man as a living unity. God did not make man to be a personal soul that merely inhabits a body, but a person who consists of a united body and soul."[8]

This is an important observation to make. Because of the influence of the materialist worldview that denies the existence of the soul—a worldview that says we're nothing but a body—some Christians have said something like, "You *have* a body, but you *are* a soul." While that was intended to fight against a real error, it is actually a swing of the pendulum in the direction of the opposite error. You are not a soul that merely possesses a body; you are a body-soul composite, a psychosomatic unity.

The image-bearing human is a person who consists of a united body and soul. So much is that the case that when the soul is separated from the body in death, Scripture speaks of the soul as if it's in an unnatural state, akin to nakedness (2 Cor. 5:1–4). In his study on the human constitution, John Flavel defined the soul as, "a vital, spiritual, and immortal substance, endowed with an understanding, will, and various affections; *created with an inclination to the body*, and infused therein by the Lord."[9] The soul is not the enemy of the body, and the body is not the prison of the soul. The soul is positively inclined to the body, and the body is the natural home of the soul.

8 Beeke and Smalley, *Reformed Systematic Theology*, 2:233.

9 John Flavel, *Pneumatologia: A Treatise on the Soul of Man, in The Works of John Flavel*, 6 vols. (Carlisle, PA: Banner of Truth, 1968), 2:495, emphasis added.

In keeping with this, Scripture places a high premium on the body, with respect to the Christian life. Believers are urged to present their bodies as a living and holy sacrifice to God, as their spiritual service of worship (Rom. 12:1). Paul specified that Christians' "bodies are members of Christ" (1 Cor. 6:15), not just their souls, so much so that Scripture says if they unite the members of their bodies to a prostitute, they will have united Christ Himself to a prostitute.

The way a Christian conducts himself in the body is of immense consequence! Just a few verses later, Paul continued, "Your body is the temple of the Holy Spirit" (6:19), which is to say that the eternal, immutable, omnipresent, holy God takes up residence in the believer's body.

On that awe-filled basis, we are commanded to glorify God in our bodies (6:20), for "the body is not for immorality, but for the Lord" (6:13). So far from a gnostic dualism that dichotomizes the soul and the body and demeans the body, Scripture teaches that the body is vital in the Christian life.

Embodied Savior, Embodied Salvation

That is only strengthened by the truth that Christ Himself became a body-soul entity when He took on human nature in His incarnation. The Word became flesh (John 1:14). All the fullness of deity dwells in Him in bodily form (Col 2:9). He bore our sins in His body on the cross (1 Pet. 2:24).

This is so central to the Christian faith that the apostle John made it a test of orthodoxy: "By this you know the Spirit of God: every spirit that confesses that Jesus Christ has come in the flesh is from God" (1 John 4:2). He stated it negatively in his second letter: "For many deceivers have gone out into the world, those who do not acknowledge Jesus Christ as coming in the flesh. This is the deceiver and the antichrist" (2 John 7).

Similarly, Paul made the bodily resurrection of Christ an essential Christian doctrine: "If Christ has not been raised, then our preaching is vain, [and] your faith also is vain. . . . If Christ has not been raised, your faith is worthless; you are still in your sins" (1 Cor. 15:14, 17).

His bodily resurrection is the ground of our bodily resurrection. Our bodies will not be cast off to rot or be left behind as the soul's prison. No, we are "waiting eagerly for . . . the redemption of our body" (Rom. 8:23), when Christ "will transform the body of our humble state into conformity with the body of His glory" (Phil 3:20–21).

For eternity, God's people will live in an embodied existence on a physical, new earth. Scripture does not describe heaven as an ethereal spiritual realm populated with disembodied spirits. It speaks of a new earth, with a new Jerusalem; with walls and gates and foundation stones; with streets and rivers and trees (Rev. 21–22).

Therefore, there is no spiritual-physical dualism in Christianity. The Bible teaches not that man is a soul who has a body, but that man is a soul and man is a body—a body-soul composite, a psychosomatic unity—from the garden of Eden to the New Jerusalem.

Consequently, embodied sexual differentiation is a good gift of God's design for humankind. Since nature is the work of a purposeful God, and since our bodies have always been a part of that nature, "there is a purpose in the physical structures of our bodies that we are called to respect."[10] Not to manipulate—as if our bodies were an impediment to our self-expression. Not to medicate, mutilate, amputate, or castrate in an attempt to subjugate our bodies to our feelings and desires. But we are to receive the body we have as a blessing, as a kind revelation from heaven that testifies truthfully to our own God-given identity. To steward and care for. To employ as a vehicle of accomplishing the will of God and of testifying to the truth of His character as His image bearers.

The Glory of Our Distinctiveness

A fifth truth about gender that Scripture reveals is the glory of our distinctiveness as male and female. The gender binary isn't just true; it's beautiful. Two main passages bear this out.

Deuteronomy 22:5

The first text is Deuteronomy 22:5. This section of the law seems to be a transition between Moses' exposition of the sixth and seventh commandments: "You shall not murder," and "You shall not commit adultery."[11] In other words, it's a section about the preservation of life (e.g., don't ignore a straying beast, 22:1–4; build a parapet on your roof, 22:8) together with laws of sexual morality (22:13ff).

So, in a flash-point between those two, verse 5 is a comment about the preservation of life by avoiding sexual immorality: "A woman shall not wear

---

10 Pearcey, *Love Thy Body*, 32.

11 Douglas F. Kelly, *Deuteronomy: A Mentor Expository Commentary* (Ross-shire, UK: Christian Focus, 2021), 299; Eugene Merrill, *Deuteronomy: An Exegetical and Theological Exposition of Holy Scripture*, NAC 4 (Nashville: B&H, 1994), 297–98.

a man's things, nor shall a man put on a woman's clothing; for whoever does these things is an abomination to Yahweh your God" (author's translation).

We can observe several things from this passage. The main point is that there are styles of dress and items of clothing and accessories that distinguish men from women. There are "things which pertain to a man" (Deut. 22:5 KJV), and there is "clothing" that is recognized as "a woman's," consistent with the cultural expressions of the time.

Now, Scripture never gives lists of precisely what clothing items "pertain to a man" versus a woman, because those things do change according to time and place. Rather, readers of Scripture are expected to know what clothes, in their time and place, pertain more to a man and more to a woman, and they are commanded to express the distinctiveness of male and female in the way they dress.

Old Testament scholar Jason DeRouchie summarized it well. He said,

> Thus, two things appear to be at stake in this law: [1] Everyone needed to let individual gender expression align with one's biological sex; and [2] Everyone needed to guard against gender confusion, so that others would not wrongly perceive a man to be a woman and a woman to be a man based on dress."[12]

In other words, men glorify God in obedience to this law when they look and speak and behave like men. And women glorify God in obedience to this law when they look and speak and behave like women.

Failure to do this is "an abomination to Yahweh your God." *Tōēvah*, a severe word, is used here. It is a term reserved for especially grave offenses against God. In Deuteronomy 13:13–14, it refers to idolatry, as the text speaks of "worthless men [who] have gone out from among [the people of God] and have seduced the inhabitants of their city, saying, 'Let us go and serve other gods.'" That is an "abomination [that] has been done among you," and it merits the death penalty.

In Deuteronomy 18:10–12, the word is used to describe divination, witchcraft, and sorcery: "Whoever does these things is detestable [or abominable] to Yahweh." It's used of homosexuality in Leviticus 18:22 and 20:13, of adultery in Deuteronomy 24:2–4, of temple prostitution in Ezekiel 16:22 and 58, and of incest in Ezekiel 22:11.

While all sin is offensive to God and violates His perfect holiness, abominations dishonor Him in a special sense. They are a contravention not only

---

12 Jason DeRouchie, *How to Understand and Apply the Old Testament: Twelve Steps from Exegesis to Theology* (Phillipsburg, NJ: P&R Publishing, 2017), 446.

of God's will, but of His very nature and design for His creatures.[13] When men present as women or women present as men, it is an abominable attack on God's design for mankind to rightly represent Him to the world as His image bearers in their distinctiveness as male and female.

If that is true of cross-dressing—just wearing the garments of the opposite sex, as Deuteronomy 22:5 discusses—how much more is it true of transgenderism, in which God's image bearers chemically and surgically alter their very bodies to reject God's good design.

First Corinthians 11:3–16

A second text is First Corinthians 11:3–16, a passage worth quoting in full.

> But I want you to understand that Christ is the head of every man, and the man is the head of a woman, and God is the head of Christ. Every man who has something on his head while praying or prophesying disgraces his head. But every woman who has her head uncovered while praying or prophesying disgraces her head, for she is one and the same as the woman whose head is shaved. For if a woman does not cover her head, let her also have her hair cut off; but if it is disgraceful for a woman to have her hair cut off or her head shaved, let her cover her head. For a man ought not to have his head covered, since he is the image and glory of God; but the woman is the glory of man. For man does not originate from woman, but woman from man; for indeed man was not created for the woman's sake, but woman for the man's sake. Therefore the woman ought to have a symbol of authority on her head, because of the angels. However, in the Lord, neither is woman independent of man, nor is man independent of woman. For as the woman originates from the man, so also the man has his birth through the woman; and all things originate from God. Judge for yourselves: is it proper for a woman to pray to God with her head uncovered? Does not even nature itself teach you that if a man has long hair, it is a dishonor to him, but if a woman has long hair, it is a glory to her? For her hair is given to her for a covering. But if one is inclined to be contentious, we have no other practice, nor have the churches of God.

This passage raises many interpretive questions, but the main point is clear: Men and women honor the glory and beauty of God's good design by presenting their own physical appearances in accordance with the distinctiveness of their biological sex. Paul uses the length of hair as an example in this passage, and says nature—that is, "the regular, established order of

---

13 Owen Strachan, *Reenchanting Humanity: A Theology of Mankind* (Ross-shire, UK: Christian Focus, 2019), 173.

things"[14]—teaches that it is "disgraceful" for a man to wear his hair in a way a woman does and for a woman to wear her hair in the way a man does.

Men should carry themselves in a masculine way and not in an effeminate way. Women should carry themselves in a feminine way and not in a masculine way. God has built this into nature, so that it is proper for men to feel shame when they embody feminine characteristics, and it is proper for women to feel shame when they embody masculine characteristics.[15] Even when it stops short of transgenderism, androgyny is a concession to this attack on God's design.

It bears repeating. Men glorify God by honoring His good design when they look, speak, and behave like men, and women glorify God by honoring His good design when they look, speak, and behave like women. And this distinctiveness is glorious. It is beautiful for men to act like men, and it is beautiful for women to act like women, because it is part of the beauty of God's design.

We appreciate the skill of an orchestra that plays a magnificent piece of music in unison. But the true beauty of music is revealed when that orchestra plays a masterpiece in harmony. Something about the unity in the midst of the distinctiveness moves beyond skillfulness and into beauty.

And that is because that unity-in-diversity represents something of the identity of God Himself. God exists in the unity of His singular nature while at the same time in the plurality of the three Persons: Father, Son, and Spirit. The Triune God is Himself the beauty behind all beauty, and that is one reason we find harmony to be more beautiful than unison. It is why there is glory in unified distinctiveness. As God's image bearers, we magnify and display that glory when we honor the distinctiveness of the gender boundaries.

---

14 Frederick W. Danker, Walter Bauer, William F. Ardnt, and F. Wilbur Gingrich, *A Greek-English Lexicon of the New Testament and Other Early Christian Literature*, electronic ed., rev. and ed. Frederick W. Danker (Chicago: University of Chicago Press, 2000).

15 Andrew David Naselli, 1 Corinthians, in *ESV Expository Commentary, Volume 10: Romans–Galatians* (Wheaton, IL: Crossway, 2020), 317.

Study Questions:

1. As mentioned in the text, in a sense, God says concerning each person's body: "*My* body, *My* choice." Do you agree with the propriety of that? Why or why not? What are some practical implications of this for your own life?

2. Why can we be sure that gender is grounded in our biological sex? How will you respond when a friend challenges that notion by claiming that sex is biological while gender is not?

3. Why are hermaphroditism and other disorders of sexual development not evidence against the gender binary?

4. Given passages like Psalm 139, how will you respond to someone who claims he or she was born in the wrong body?

5. What truths about God's character can someone meditate on to help him or her recognize that He is trustworthy, even in the midst of gender dysphoria?

6. How does an atheistic view of nature contribute to transgender ideology? What is the biblical response?

7. True or False: "You have a body, but you are a soul." Explain why you chose your answer.

8. Discuss the several different ways in which Christianity holds the human body in high esteem.

9. Given the centrality of the body to human identity, when people feel a disconnect between their internal feelings and their outward physical characteristics, what should they do?

10. What are the implications of Deuteronomy 22:5 and First Corinthians 11:3–16 for transgenderism? For those who portray male effeminacy and female masculinity?

4

Practical Counsel on Transgenderism

IN LIGHT OF THE BIBLICAL teaching on gender presented in the previous chapter, I want to offer words of counsel to those who struggle with transgenderism in different ways.

To the Unbeliever who Struggles

First, to those who do not yet trust in Jesus and struggle with feelings of gender dysphoria: I can't imagine the weight, the burden, and the fear that accompany feeling trapped in the body of the wrong gender. I am genuinely sorry for the turmoil you're experiencing. But you can be certain that if God, your Creator, made you a man, He did it on purpose, according to His wise and loving design. Because of that, it is glorious and beautiful for you to be a man. And if God, your Creator, has made you a woman, He did it on purpose, according to His wise and loving design. Because of that, it is glorious and beautiful for you to be a woman.

Even if it feels like things don't make sense—even if you're a man who feels like stereotypically masculine things are strange and unnatural, it doesn't mean you're not a man. Even if you're a woman who feels stereotypically feminine things are awkward and out of place, it doesn't mean you're not a woman.

All of life, friend, is about honoring, glorifying, and worshipping God. Life is about His glory, His esteem, and His fame—not our own. Satisfaction, fulfillment, and lasting pleasure are found only in exalting Him. God means to get glory from you in the precise way that He made you—as a man or a woman. You cannot honor Him as He's designed by seeking to alter your gender. Men can only glorify God as men. And women can only glorify God as women.

The good news is that you may enjoy the freedom found in glorifying God as He's designed you to be. We find such freedom in Jesus Christ. Jesus calls to Himself those wearied by sin: "Come to Me, all who are weary and heavy-laden, and I will give you rest" (Matt. 11:28). You who languish under the unbearable burden of your sin may come to Christ for rest. Elsewhere, He says, "If the Son makes you free, you will be free indeed" (John 8:36).

Friend, you are a sinner, you have offended God by your sin, and you come short of His holiness. Like the rest of us, you don't deserve to go to heaven. But like the rest of us, Jesus will have you, if you turn from your sin, and put your trust in Him. He has lived, died, and risen again so that sinners may find rest, forgiveness, cleansing, and righteousness in Him.

Come to Christ and find life. You might pray something like this: "Lord Jesus, I am so conflicted. I feel like I'm in the wrong body, and it is so tiresome. Your Word tells me that I am to live in accordance with my biological sex, but it seems so unnatural. But Lord, I have nowhere else to turn. You alone have the words of eternal life, and You alone can make me free. Please break the bonds of the sin that enslaves me. Please conform my thinking and my feelings to the truth, so that I can have a sense of myself as You see me, rather than the false identity I've deceived myself into seeing. I confess that false identity as sin. I desire to turn from that lifestyle. I repudiate it, and I want nothing more to do with it. I trust you for forgiveness. Please give me grace to follow after You in obedience."

HELPING YOUR CHILD

Perhaps you don't struggle with temptations related to transgenderism, but your child does. As you counsel your child, they must understand that it is good for boys to be boys and girls to be girls.

Sometimes, if a boy is sensitive, gentle, and emotional, other kids make fun of him, saying he is "girly." They may call him "gay," or even insist that he must really be a girl on the inside. If a girl is tough, resilient, and assertive, she's told she's a tomboy or butch and that maybe she's really a boy on the inside. Those are lies, and it is important for children to hear their parents dismiss such nonsense as lies.

That's not to say that there aren't aspects of a child's character that may need to change. Boys may need to be encouraged to rule their emotions (Prov. 16:32) and cultivate strength (1 Kings 2:2; 1 Cor. 16:13). Girls may need to be taught to be more deferential and cultivate a softer disposition (1 Pet. 3:4). But no one should conform his or her body to match feelings.

If anything, people need to conform their feelings to match the outward, objective fact of their bodies.

Parents, teach your children that our hearts are deceitful and desperately wicked (Jer. 17:9). Teach them that their bodies are not lying to them, but their hearts are. Insist that they not attempt to construct a fantasy life by trying to change objective facts to suit subjective feelings. Rather, exhort them to receive God's kind revelation of objective facts, and to bring those facts to bear on their subjective feelings.

When that happens—especially for children—research indicates that feelings of gender dysphoria usually subside naturally. According to the DSM-V, "as many as 98% of gender confused boys and 88% of gender confused girls eventually accept their biological sex after naturally passing through puberty."[1] That means parents should not affirm a child's gender nonconformity in any way. They should not allow a child to live in ways out of accord with his or her God-given gender. And the very last thing anyone should do is let a child take puberty blockers or other hormones that can lead to long-term physical damage and irreversible harm.

Children need to hear that everyone feels uncomfortable in their own bodies at times, partially due to the way sin has corrupted the entire world. They need to hear about the remedy for sin in Christ, and that no discomfort is an indication that they're trapped in the body of the wrong gender.

A boy needs his parents to tell him it's wonderful that God made him a boy, that they are proud of the young man he's growing into, and that they love to see him growing in strength, in taking responsibility, and in his desire to protect others.

A girl needs her parents to tell her that it's wonderful that God made her a girl, that she is a beautiful young woman, and they love to see her growing in her gentle and quiet spirit, in her helpfulness around the house, and in her desire to nurture others.

Every child needs to know he or she can glorify God uniquely as the boy or girl that He has fearfully and wonderfully made him or her to be. Children need to know their parents are fully committed to helping them glorify God in the way He has made them.

---

1 American Psychiatric Association, *Diagnostic and Statistical Manual of Mental Disorders*, 5th ed. (Arlington, VA: American Psychiatric Association, 2013), 451–59. See American College of Pediatricians, "Gender Ideology Harms Children," https://acpeds.org/assets/imported/9.14.17-Gender-Ideology-Harms-Children_updated-MC.pdf (accessed December 2023).

PREFERRED PRONOUNS

Church members often ask me whether or not they should use someone's preferred pronouns or an alternate name that does not match the person's biological gender. The Christian's only answer is in Second Corinthians 13:8: "We can do nothing against the truth, but only for the truth."

To use pronouns out of accord with someone's actual gender is to lie to that person. It is to affirm them in their delusion and rebellion, and it positively reinforces their sin, which must be confessed, repented of, and forsaken. It is to act against the truth and cannot be squared with Christian conviction.

But don't people have the right to go by whatever name they want? My given name is Michael, but I go by Mike. Others use a middle name rather than their first name. Still others have a nickname. Some people even legally change their names from those on their birth certificates. If it doesn't violate biblical principles to call others by a preferred name, why should that be the case for a transgender person?

Because the intent behind those other name changes has nothing to do with contravening God's design. In transgenderism, even if a man legally changes his name, the intent behind the name change is to obscure his God-given identity as a man. To refer to him by a feminine or even ambiguous name is to lie to that man, to encourage him in his rebellious delusion, and to act against the truth.

We must heed Paul's admonition, "Do not lie to one another, since you laid aside the old self with its evil practices" (Col. 3:9). Lying is an evil practice, and the follower of Christ must lay it aside.

WHAT ABOUT LOVE?

Some people ask: "What about love? Isn't the primary Christian virtue love? Didn't Jesus say the world will know we're His disciples by our love?"

Yes, but biblical, Christian love is not unconditional affirmation. First John 2:15 says, "Do not love the world nor the things in the world. If anyone loves the world, the love of the Father is not in him." This sort of love of the world is mutually exclusive with loving God.

James says that very thing: "Friendship with the world is enmity with God" (James 4:4). Christians are to love, but we are to speak the truth in love (Eph. 4:15), because love "does not rejoice in unrighteousness, but rejoices with the truth" (1 Cor. 13:6). Therefore, you cannot love people by lying to them. Neither can you love people while helping them lie to themselves and others. I appreciate the quote: "To affirm a sinful lifestyle built on lies is not love; it is cowardice."[2]

Love cannot affirm what harms and destroys. In his excellent book, *When Harry Became Sally*, Ryan Anderson recounts the story of a woman who called herself "Crash," started taking testosterone at 20 years old and then detransitioned at 27. What's so striking about her testimony is how clearly she realized that those who affirmed her in her desire to transition had harmed her, even though they were trying to be helpful and affirming. She says her doctor

> hurt me, helped me hurt myself. That definitely wasn't her intention but that's still what happened. This contradiction is difficult to face and understand. She treated me like I wanted to be treated at the time. She was supporting me and helping me do what I was convinced was best for me and I appreciated that a lot. . . . And now when I look back I'm horrified and creeped out. There's something disturbing about doing something you think is good for yourself but that turns out to be really self-destructive and it's even worse when so many other people were helping you and making it easier for you to do it. It's hard enough taking in how I managed to hurt myself when I was trying to find happiness and express my true self. How am I supposed to deal with how all these people in my life were trying to be helpful but were actually enabling? . . . I did trust my [healthcare] providers (as much as I can trust any medical professional) and they helped me destroy myself. . . . You thought you were doing good but you were giving me tools to hurt myself. I thought I needed to come to you to get what I needed to be happy but I was wrong. We both had no idea what we were doing, what was really going on. Your good will didn't end my suffering, it increased it. . . . Your kindness led to more scars, not less.[3]

This testimony illustrates the profound point that love is not unconditional affirmation. Even if someone believes she is pursuing her greatest self-fulfillment, it is not love to affirm her in her self-destruction.

True love seeks the objective benefit of the beloved. Sometimes, what is good for someone is just plain contrary to what they want. As Christians, we must be courageous enough to love well, even when it means crossing someone's deeply felt desires.

---

2 MacArthur and Busenitz (eds.), "Identity Crisis," 116.

3 Anderson, *When Harry Became Sally*, 60–61.

To the Believer who Struggles

To the believer who struggles with desires to express himself or herself contrary to biological gender—to the one who knows that such desires are sinful and incompatible with following Jesus, to the one who aches to be rid of these desires—remember the good news of Calvary. Your Substitute bore your sins in His body on the cross and there declared that all was finished (John 19:30). He put away sin by the sacrifice of Himself (Heb. 9:26). He has canceled the certificate of debt consisting of decrees against us, having nailed it to the cross (Col. 2:14).

Because He did, He looks upon you, Christian, and says, "Such *were* some of you, but you were washed" (1 Cor. 6:9–11). That may have been your identity in another life, but you have died, and your life is hidden with Christ in God (Col. 3:3). If anyone is in Christ, he is a new creation. The old things passed away; behold, new things have come (2 Cor. 5:17). You have been crucified with Christ, and it is no longer you who live, but Christ lives in you (Gal. 2:20).

Christ is your life (Col. 3:4). He is your identity now. And there is grace enough in Him to subdue every sin, to defang the most devilish lust. "Those who belong to Christ Jesus have crucified the flesh with its passions and desires" (Gal. 5:24). Sin shall no longer be your master, because you are not under the law that keeps you in bondage; you are under the grace that frees the captives from their slavery (Rom. 6:14–18).

Yes, you were born into this cursed world with fallen and corrupt desires. But friend, if you're trusting in Jesus, you were born again from the blessed world above and made alive in Christ (1 John 5:1). Though your progress may feel painfully slow, you are being transformed into the image of Christ, day by day, hour by hour, as you fix your eyes on Him and behold His glory by faith (2 Cor. 3:18). That glorious sight of Him will strengthen you to make war on the fleshly desires that remain, and put to death what is earthly in you (Rom. 8:12–13, Col. 3:5).

As those sinful thoughts and desires arise in your heart, you have the power to seize them, to confess them as sin, to bring them to the Lord and to this gospel, and to turn away from them.

"Even so, consider yourselves dead to sin and alive to God in Christ Jesus" (Rom. 6:11). Consider yourselves this way! Preach to yourself, "No, these desires are not me."

They won't go down without a fight. It's as if sin says, "What do you mean they're not you? These internal desires are precisely what tells who you are!" But fight back: "No, they're not! They may have been the old me, but that one has been crucified! I've been given a new identity! I am dead to that and alive to God! That is not who I am or who I've been recreated to be."

After you've preached to yourself, pray for help: "Lord, give grace, that I might walk in the strength of what You've purchased for me. Give me the grace to bring my practice in line with my position."

This is the war that every Christian fights, no matter what his or her temptations are. And there is grace in Christ for victory.

A CALL TO REPENTANCE AND FAITH

Ultimately, we must turn our eyes away from the dark caverns of our own deceitful hearts and set them upon the character of our God. God is God; you and I are not.

To the reader who remains outside of Christ and may not be struggling with transgenderism but is struggling with any sin—dear sinner, lay down your arms. No matter how persistent your rebellion, you cannot overcome the omnipotent God who created you. Turn away from your self-exaltation, and your desire to put yourself in the place of God, and bow your knee in humble submission before Him, acknowledging Him as the rightful Sovereign and Lord of your life.

God is not only the sovereign Lord; He is a wise God. His thoughts are not your thoughts, and His ways are not your ways (Isa. 55:8). You have devised and schemed and convinced yourself of the wisdom of your own worldview, which raises itself up against the knowledge of God as revealed in His Word (2 Cor. 10:5). But God has made foolish the wisdom of this world (1 Cor. 1:20), for "the wisdom of this world is foolishness before God" (1 Cor. 3:19). Whether you reject His thoughts on the matter of gender and sexuality, or on any other matter He reveals in His Word, you must turn away from that vain conceit whereby you would exalt yourself above the omniscient God, submit your mind to His revelation, and confess that His ways are wisest.

Further, God is not only sovereign and wise, but He is also good. He is trustworthy. He is the God whose ultimate self-revelation is the Lord Jesus, who calls you: "Come to Me, all who are weary and heavy-laden, and I will give you rest."

You who labor under the burden of your sin, come to Christ for rest! There is sufficient grace in Him to conquer every rebel power at work in you. Whether you are, as First Corinthians 6 says, a fornicator, an idolater, an adulterer, an effeminate one, a homosexual, a thief, a coveter, a drunkard, a reviler, or a swindler, it may be spoken of you as it was of those believers: "Such *were* some of you; but you were washed, but you were sanctified, but you were justified in the name of the Lord Jesus Christ and in the Spirit of our God."

This gospel that washes, sanctifies, and justifies remains free and offered to you, because the blood and righteousness of the Savior remains worthy. His blood has satisfied divine wrath for His people; His righteousness has quieted the law's awful demands; and forgiveness is yours for the taking. Turn away from your sins and trust in Christ for your salvation.

Study Questions:

1. What would you say to an unbelieving friend who feels trapped in the body of the wrong gender?

2. What should parents tell their young son who has begun wondering if he's "really a girl"? What should they tell their young daughter who has begun wondering if she's "really a boy"?

3. According to the DSM-V, what percentage of gender confused boys and girls eventually accept their biological gender after passing naturally through puberty? What implications does that have for what curricula citizens should allow in their public schools?

4. Would you respect someone's request to refer to them by pronouns that do not accord with their biological gender? How about a name that is designed to obscure their biological gender? What biblical passages shape your answer?

5. What do you think of Crash's testimony, that those who thought they were helping were actually hurting her?

6. How would you counsel a believing friend who struggles with feelings of gender dysphoria?

5

Same-Sex Mirage

Why Christians Cannot Affirm Homosexuality

MANY BELIEVERS HAVE close friends and family members who are being swept away in the sea of sexual perversion in which our society is drowning. And though many Christians are faithful to communicate Scripture's condemnation of homosexuality, their loved ones have objections, retorts, and rebuttals. They reject the notion that homosexuality is a sin. "It's not our business to tell people who they can love!" "Jesus never condemned homosexuality!" "We need to love and affirm all people!" The culture catechizes its disciples very effectively.

That means believers, as faithful ambassadors of our King, must be equipped to respond to those arguments and to engage unbelievers with the truth. In this chapter, I offer biblical responses to five popular arguments the world gives for why homosexuality is reconcilable with biblical Christianity.

My goal is for you to be equipped to have loving, patient, compassionate, and truthful discussions with your loved ones, so you can bring the law of God and the gospel of Christ to bear on their consciences, and, if God would be gracious, see them repent and believe in Jesus.

Why Should You Even Care?

The first argument is usually advanced in the form of a question: "Why do Christians care about what two consenting adults do in their bedroom?"

The quick answer is: because the triune God is the Lord of all. This is His universe, we are accountable to Him, and His law is to be the rule of our lives. He tells us that the only context in which we are to express sexual intimacy is in the covenant of marriage.

Then the objection comes back, "Well, plenty of homosexuals want to be married. But you're against that too! Why should you care about who marries whom? If two people want to make a commitment to each other for life, why shouldn't they have the right to do that?"

God Says So

The first answer to that question is that the Bible unambiguously declares that homosexuality is sinful. Leviticus 18:22 says, "You shall not lie with a male as one lies with a female; it is an abomination." First Corinthians 6:9–10 says that fornicators, idolaters, adulterers, effeminate, and homosexuals will not inherit the kingdom of God. Romans 1:25–27 describes homosexuality as a degrading passion, unnatural, and indecent.

Like all other sins, then, the wages of unrepentant homosexuality is death (Rom. 6:23)—eternal separation from God (Matt. 25:46; 2 Thess. 1:9). And since the purpose of the civil government is to restrain evil and promote the well-being of society, the government should not sanction and incentivize what the Lord of the universe expressly forbids and promises will lead to eternal punishment.

A second answer is that God Himself is the Creator of marriage. He performed the first marriage (Gen. 2:18), and the Designer of marriage defines it as being between only one man and one woman. Since God is the Lord of the universe, we must accept His Word. Genesis 2 says that when God purposed to make a suitable companion who was complementary to Adam, He did not make another man from Adam's rib. Instead, He fashioned a woman. In God's mind, only a woman was "a helper suitable for" man (Gen. 2:18).

Jesus reaffirmed this design. When a Pharisee asked Jesus about marriage and divorce, it was no accident that the Son of God prefaced His response by underscoring that God made humanity as "male and female" (Matt. 19:4–5).

God did not make man only male, or only female. He designed that a man would leave his family and be joined to his wife and that these two would become one flesh (Gen. 2:24). Jesus didn't speak of a man leaving his parents to be joined to his husband, but his wife. So, the very definition of marriage from the Creator of marriage—and thus the sole infallible authority on marriage—is that it is between one man and one woman.

Marriage: A Parable of the Gospel

But why has God defined marriage this way? The answer to this question gets to the heart of why Christians care about who marries whom. Marriage is a glorious institution, but not in and of itself. God has designed marriage to be a symbol, picture, or parable that points to something greater than marriage: to the gospel of Jesus Christ. The purpose of marriage is to bring glory to God by magnifying the relationship of covenant-keeping grace that exists between Christ and His Bride, the church.[1]

The apostle Paul taught this in Ephesians 5:22–33, where he gave the most extended instruction on marriage in all of Scripture. He quoted from the first wedding sermon, just as Jesus did (Gen. 2:24; Matt. 19:4–5), and immediately followed that by saying, "This mystery is great; but I am speaking with reference to Christ and the church" (Eph. 5:32). Paul spoke about marriage with reference to Christ and the church.

In this passage, Paul laid out God's master plan for marriage: the husband's loving headship (5:25–30) and the wife's respectful submission (5:22–24). The reasons Paul gave for His commands concerning these marital roles are striking:

- "Wives, be subject to your own husbands, as to the Lord. *For* the husband is the head of the wife, *as Christ also* is the head of the church, He Himself being the Savior of the body. But *as the church* is subject to Christ, *so also the wives* ought to be to their husbands in everything" (emphasis mine).
- Husbands, love your wives, *just as Christ also* loved the church and gave Himself up for her . . . for no one ever hated his own flesh, but nourishes and cherishes it, *just as Christ also* does the church" (emphasis mine).

The basis for every one of Paul's commands concerning marriage is the work of Christ in His relationship with the church. This is because marriage is a parable of the gospel. It exists to illustrate the way Christ keeps the covenant commitment that He made to *His* bride—to save her, to purify her, and to glorify her in His presence (Eph. 5:26–27).

By His sacrificial death, Jesus saved His people from sin, from God's wrath, from just punishment, from fruitlessness, and from a wasted life. He took our sin out of the way so His people can enjoy fellowship with their Creator and Redeemer forever. Marriage is purposely designed to display the glory of that good news.

But marriage only glorifies the gospel insofar as the husband accurately pictures Christ and as the wife accurately pictures the church. This, ultimately, is why Bible-believing Christians must be opposed to homosexual

1 John Piper, *This Momentary Marriage: A Parable of Permanence* (Wheaton, IL: Crossway, 2009).

unions: because it mars the picture of that precious gospel that marriage is designed to be. If marriage is given to mankind to point to the truth concerning Christ's covenant-keeping grace with His people, and if the husband pictures Christ and the wife pictures the church, then any tampering with those participants hopelessly confuses and fatally obfuscates the gospel.

Christ is "the head of the church" and "the Savior of the body" (Eph. 5:23). But what would a so-called "marriage" between two men communicate about the gospel? That Christ lovingly leads, serves, and saves only Himself. That is not good news, because in that case, the church would be left to herself to deal with her sin.

Alternatively, what would a "marriage" between two women communicate about the gospel? That the church should follow, and respect, and submit to only herself. But there's no gospel there either, because that's a picture of trusting in ourselves for salvation. The church submitting to no one but herself doesn't illustrate loving dependence upon a sufficient Savior, but only self-righteousness and self-effort.

Marriage, according to its design as a picture of the gospel, only makes sense when the husband's servant leadership pictures Christ's loving headship over His people and when the wife's respectful submission pictures the church's joyful submission to her Lord. This is the principal reason Bible-believing Christians oppose homosexual "marriage." It's not ultimately about tax law, labels, or the culture wars. It's about the gospel—that precious message through which our sins are forgiven and through which our Savior reconciles us to God.

PICKING AND CHOOSING?

A second argument used by those aiming to reconcile homosexuality with Christianity is what I call the "Picking and Choosing" objection. These people observe that the Bible gives many commands, especially in the Old Testament, that Christians don't follow today—like the prohibition against mixing fabrics (Lev. 19:19) or eating shellfish and pork (Lev. 11:7–11). In their minds, we disobey those texts while we insist on obeying prohibitions against homosexuality. "You pick and choose which commands to obey or disobey based on the sins you like or don't like," they say.

Unbiblical Reasoning

In the first place, this reasoning is patently unbiblical. Even if unstated, this argument concedes that the Bible does condemn homosexuality. The objector is simply contending that we should ignore more of what the Bible clearly commands. "You disobey God's Word all the time. Why should disobeying His commands against homosexuality be any different?"

But we must say forcefully: Christians do not think this way about God's Word. Those who love God do not seek to legitimize disobedience to Him. The Word of God is the delight of the child of God (Jer. 15:16). We should say to those reasoning this way: "If you feel you have to explain away God's Word, you are behaving more like His enemy than His child."

The Law Sets God's People Apart

Second, this objection fails to understand the purposes of the Mosaic law and how the Christian under the new covenant should relate to the law that was given under the old covenant. For one thing, the ceremonial regulations of the Mosaic law were designed to set Israel apart from all the other nations. No other nation cared about eating animals that didn't chew cud or wearing clothes woven with two different fabrics. No other nation allowed a perfectly good day of work (and profits) slip through their fingers by resting on Saturday. In all these restrictions, God's design was for His people to be different than all the nations, because He was different than the gods of the nations.

In the present age, though, God's people are no longer bound by physical, national, or even cultural boundaries. The church is not a civil government or a theocracy, but a spiritual building (Eph. 2:21). Because of that, we're not set apart by obeying laws about fabrics, foods, and feast days; we're set apart by our moral purity and holiness of life. We are to come out from all moral impurity and be separate, because the Holy God of heaven dwells in us and walks among us (2 Cor. 6:16–17).

So, one function of the Mosaic law was to set God's people apart in tangible, physical ways in order to show His own uniqueness.

The Law Points God's People to a Savior

But the law was also given to Israel for another purpose: to illustrate God's standard of righteousness, to show how far short of that standard His people fall, and ultimately, to point them to a Savior who would accomplish that righteousness on their behalf.

Disobedience to God's law demanded a punishment, but God graciously instituted a sacrificial system in which His people's sin was punished in a substitute. The bloody exercise of animal sacrifice made it unmistakable that God was infinitely holy and that sin was deadly serious. Day after day, year after year, all of Israel offered sacrifices for their sins. The lesson would be indelibly impressed upon their minds: They could not live the way God required; He was holy, and they were hopelessly unholy.

Because of this, Paul called the law a tutor or a schoolmaster.

> But the Scripture has shut up everyone under sin, so that the promise by faith in Jesus Christ might be given to those who believe. But before faith came, we were kept in custody under the law, being shut up to the faith which was later to be revealed. Therefore the Law has become our tutor to lead us to Christ, so that we may be justified by faith. (Gal. 3:22–24)

The Law was designed to teach Israel that they could never meet God's standard of holiness and had to look to God alone to receive His righteousness by grace. In the fullness of time, God provided that righteousness in the person of Jesus Christ (Gal. 4:4–5; Rom. 3:21–26). The law was designed to point to Him.

That's why Jesus could declare that all foods were clean (Mark 7:19) and could work on the Sabbath (Luke 6:2): The Son of Man is Lord of the Sabbath (Matt 12:8). It's why God's people no longer offer sacrifices in a temple: In Jesus, something greater than the temple is here (Matt. 12:6). Access to God is no longer mediated by the ceremonial regulations of the Mosaic covenant but by those of a new covenant (Jer. 31:31–34; Luke 22:20), whose mediator was not a temple or a priest, but the Son of God Himself (Heb. 9:15).

This is also why the book of Hebrews declared the Mosaic covenant to be "obsolete" (Heb. 8:13)—because the purpose for which that covenant was given was fulfilled in Christ. The entire point of the dietary laws was: Trust in Jesus. God's people are no longer set apart by not mixing fabrics but by being united to Jesus by faith and following Him in holiness.

No Longer Under a Tutor

Christians can mix fabrics or eat pork, then, not because we can pick and choose which commands to follow. It's not that the Levitical laws were just cultural, and since our culture is different, the commands can change. Those commands aren't culturally conditioned but covenantally conditioned.

Those ceremonial commands of the Mosaic covenant have been fulfilled in Christ, the mediator of a new and better covenant. That's why Paul said in that same passage, "Therefore the Law has become our tutor to lead us to Christ, so that we may be justified by faith. But now that faith has come, we are no longer under a tutor" (Gal. 3:24–25).

Christians are not under the tutor of the Mosaic law. So, for us to attempt to keep the dietary laws and other aspects of ceremonial worship would be to deny that Jesus' righteous life and substitutionary death was sufficient to accomplish our righteousness. This is why Paul spoke so severely about professing believers who received the ceremonial rite of circumcision (Gal. 5:2).

When Christians exercise freedom to mix fabrics or to eat shellfish and pork, we are not disobeying the Mosaic law. Instead, we are living obediently in light of its fulfillment in Christ (Rom. 3:31).

Fulfilled Ceremonies vs. Abiding Moral Principles

However, the commandments against homosexuality do not belong to the ceremonial stipulations of an obsolete covenant from a bygone era. The prohibitions of homosexuality in Leviticus 18:22 and 20:13 are not repealed but repeated in the New Testament, which is God's revelation for those living under the new covenant.

Romans 1:26–27 speaks of both male and female homosexuality as instances of "degrading passions," of being "unnatural" and "indecent," an "error" worthy of a "penalty." First Corinthians 6:9–10 says that unrepentant effeminate people and homosexuals will not inherit the kingdom of God. First Timothy 1:9–10 includes "homosexuals" among "those who are lawless and rebellious," "ungodly and sinners," "unholy and profane," and "contrary to sound teaching."[2]

While the New Testament declared the fulfillment (and therefore the end) of the civil and ceremonial laws of the Mosaic covenant, these new covenant Scriptures reaffirmed the Old Testament prohibition against homosexuality, showing that it wasn't binding only upon national Israel, but also upon the new covenant people of God. The commands against homosexuality weren't designed to teach a temporary lesson, as the food laws were. No, in all ages, homosexuality tragically distorts the picture of the

2 In this passage, Paul seemed to exposit the Ten Commandments, treating "immoral men and homosexuals" in the place of the seventh commandment (Exod. 20:14), showing that Paul regarded homosexuality to be a violation of the intent of the prohibition of adultery: "Realizing the fact that law is not made for a righteous person, but for those who are lawless and rebellious, for the ungodly and sinners, for the unholy and profane, for those who kill their fathers or mothers [fifth commandment], for murderers [sixth Commandment] and immoral men and homosexuals [seventh commandment] and kidnappers [eighth commandment] and liars and perjurers [ninth commandment], and whatever else is contrary to sound teaching" (1 Tim. 1:9–10).

gospel that marriage is designed to be. On the authority of God's own Word to His people, a person cannot be in a right relationship with God through Jesus Christ while living an unrepentant homosexual lifestyle.

But you certainly can be rescued from that lifestyle by repenting from the sin of homosexuality and trusting in Jesus. First Corinthians 6:11 says that some in the Corinthian church had been homosexuals: "Such were some of you; but you were washed, but you were sanctified, but you were justified in the name of the Lord Jesus Christ in the Spirit of our God."

The homosexuals in Corinth had been cleansed. Their sins were forgiven—not by pretending their sins weren't sins, but by owning and confessing them, and by turning from them, forsaking them, and trusting in Christ's righteousness alone for acceptance with God.

That is what we preach to our loved ones. Homosexuality is indeed a sin against God and calls for His judgment, but homosexuals, along with the rest of us sinners, can be washed by the blood of the Lamb shed for the forgiveness of sins.

IS "HOMOSEXUALS" A MISTRANSLATION?

The Bible's condemnation of homosexuality is undeniable to the honest reader of Scripture (Rom. 1:25–27; 1 Cor. 6:9–11; 1 Tim. 1:9–10). However, some argue that these clear passages have been mistranslated. They claim that the word translated "homosexuals" in these New Testament texts (*arsenokoitēs*) doesn't refer to so-called "healthy," "monogamous," "committed same-sex relationships," but "abusive male-male" relationships, like pederasty and prostitution. So, they argue, when the New Testament condemns *arsenokoitēs,* it doesn't condemn all homosexuality but only certain forms of homosexual behavior that are especially perverse.

But the notion that *arsenokoitēs* is mistranslated is simply false. Etymologically, *arsenokoitēs* is a compound word formed from the term *arsēn* ("male") and *koitē* ("bed"). *Koitē* is the noun form of the verb *keimai,* which means "to lie with," in the sense of sexual intimacy. In fact, *koitē* is borrowed into Latin to make the term *coitus,* which we borrow in English as a technical biological term to describe sexual intercourse.

A literal gloss for *arsenokoitēs*, then, would be "male-bedding"—that is, a man going to bed with a man. Nothing in the word itself suggests its meaning should be restricted to a particular kind of going to bed with a man; it speaks of homosexual behavior in general.

Interestingly, *arsenokoitēs* doesn't exist in Greek literature before the New Testament. It is found in secular Greek literature after the New Testament, but it's evident that Paul coined the term himself. Where did he come up with it? Well, he got it from his Bible: the Septuagint, the Greek translation of the Old Testament. The constituent parts of *arsenokoitēs* are found in the two passages of the Levitical law that discuss homosexuality:

> Leviticus 18:22: "You shall not lie with a male as one lies with a female; it is an abomination" (Septuagint: *Kai meta <u>arsenos</u> ou koimēthēsē <u>koitēn</u> gunaikos*).
>
> Leviticus 20:13: "If there is a man who lies with a male as those who lie with a woman, both of them have committed a detestable act; they shall surely be put to death" (Septuagint: *Kai hos an koimēthē meta <u>arsenos</u> <u>koitēn</u> gunaikos*).

Both *arsenos* and *koitēn* appear in Leviticus 18:22, and in Leviticus 20:13, they appear consecutively. It's plain, then, where Paul found the term *arsenokoitēs*: he got it from the holiness code in Leviticus. Whatever Moses meant when he wrote those commandments in the law, Paul meant the same in the New Testament epistles.

There is no question: The Jews understood Moses' prohibition to refer to homosexuality in its totality. For one thing, the rabbis used the original Hebrew expression found in Leviticus 18:22 and 20:13—*mishkav zākûr*, "lying with a male"—to speak of male-male intercourse in the broadest sense. Commenting on these passages, the Talmud explicitly says the male with whom a man lays may be "an adult or minor."[3] That rules out the claim that *arsenokoitēs* refers only to pederasty.

Besides this, first-century Greek speakers understood the Mosaic prohibition in the same way. For example, the historian Josephus explained to Gentiles that "the law [of Moses] recognizes only sexual intercourse that is according to nature, that which is with a woman. . . . But it abhors the intercourse of males with males."[4] New Testament scholar Robert Gagnon commented, "There are no limitations placed on the prohibition as regards age, slave status, idolatrous context, or exchange of money. The only limitation is the sex of the participants."[5] Thus, Paul intended to reproduce the prohibition exactly as it was intended in the

---

3 *The Babylonian Talmud*, Sanhedrin 54a.

4 Flavius Josephus, *Against Apion*, 2.199.

5 This quote is from Dr. Robert Gagnon's Facebook page, posted on April 26, 2015, http://www.facebook.com/robert.a.gagnon.56/posts/10155637933520045. This comment is also cited in Pearcey, *Love Thy Body*, 308n71.

Old Testament, and the Old Testament intent was to speak of homosexuality indiscriminately.

Further, if Paul intended his condemnation to refer to a subset of homosexual practice, he wouldn't have had to coin a new term. There were Greek words for pederasty (*paiderastai, paidomanai,* and *paidophthoroi*), but rather than employ those, he coined his own compound word from the Levitical law's prohibition of homosexuality in general.

Historical sources tell us that Paul's coined word caught on, and the term *arsenokoitēs* and its cognates in post-New Testament writings—in several selections of Eusebius' writings, for example—are applied exclusively to male-male intercourse, not limited to pederasty or cult prostitution.[6] And further, when the New Testament was translated into Latin, Syriac, and Coptic, those translators all rendered *arsenokoitēs* in ways that are unambiguously translated to "men lying with men."

Besides all of that, in interpreting *arsenokoitēs,* we must also consider Paul's explicit indictment of both male and female homosexual behavior in Romans 1:26–27. There, Paul spoke in the broadest possible terms, not limiting himself to non-abusive or unloving homosexual unions. He simply spoke of women burning in their desire for women and men committing indecent acts with men.

The only objection would be to claim that Paul condemned homosexuality in general in Romans 1, only then to coin a technical term from the text of Leviticus to refer to a more specific subset of homosexual behavior in First Corinthians 6. That violates just about every principle of grammatical-historical exegesis that there is. And it clearly reveals an agenda on the part of the interpreter. Such is an interpretation in search of justification, rather than an honest, unprejudiced, objective search for the author's intent.

DID JESUS SAY NOTHING ABOUT HOMOSEXUALITY?

A fourth argument stipulates that the Old Testament law, and even Paul in the New Testament, condemned homosexuality as sinful, but objects that the Old Testament was outdated and that Paul had corrupted the way of life and the ideology that Jesus came to propagate. Christians follow Jesus, not Moses or Paul, and in His entire ministry, challengers say, Jesus said nothing at all about homosexuality. Conservative Christians are accused of making more of an issue out of homosexuality than Jesus did.

6 Robert A. J. Gagnon, *The Bible and Homosexual Practice: Texts and Hermeneutics* (Nashville: Abingdon Press, 2001), 317–23.

But is it true that Jesus never said anything about homosexuality? This objection simply does not hold up to scrutiny for at least four reasons.[7] In the first place, it's an argument from silence, a logical fallacy. Therefore, it rests on an unstable rational foundation. Jesus also didn't say a word about pedophilia, bestiality, or rape. But it would be beyond absurd to garner support for any of those abominable acts on the basis of such silence.

Jesus' silence is no more an endorsement of homosexuality than His silence on pedophilia, bestiality, incest, rape, child molestation, and any number of heinous sexual sins is an endorsement of them.

Second, a great portion of Jesus' ministry related to Israel and those familiar with the Mosaic law. They lived in an age under the Mosaic covenant, which, as we've seen, explicitly condemned homosexuality. Jesus taught that the Old Testament was breathed out by the Holy Spirit (Matt. 22:43); that it was infallible and inerrant (John 10:35); and that it was so abidingly authoritative that not the smallest stroke would pass away (Matt. 5:18). Unless some precipitating issue would force Jesus to comment on homosexuality, the only reasonable conclusion is that His view of homosexuality was the Old Testament's view of homosexuality.

Third, when Jesus did speak about marriage, He affirmed it as an institution between a male and a female. In Matthew 19, the Pharisees asked Him about divorce, hoping to trap Him into disagreeing with Moses, so they could find a reason to condemn Him. Jesus responded,

> Have you not read that He who created them from the beginning MADE THEM MALE AND FEMALE, and said, 'FOR THIS REASON A MAN SHALL LEAVE HIS FATHER AND MOTHER AND BE JOINED TO HIS WIFE, AND THE TWO SHALL BECOME ONE FLESH'? So they are no longer two, but one flesh. What therefore God has joined together, let no man separate. (Matt. 19:4–5)

If Jesus wanted to answer the Pharisees' question about divorce simply and efficiently, He could have skipped immediately to verse five: "Have you not read that the two become one flesh?" That's the answer to the question about divorce. God joins spouses together as one flesh, and man shouldn't separate what God has joined together. Why does He start by reminding the Pharisees that God made human beings male and female—something that seems beside the point? Well, He did so to make it clear that the divinely-ordained institution of marriage exists only between one

7 This section is further developed in Michael Riccardi, "WWJD about LGBT?: Evaluating LGBT Claims in Light of Christ's Teaching," *The Master's Seminary Journal*, 28/2 (Fall 2017): 167–80.

man and one woman. The fact that God created humans as male and female is inextricably linked to the institution of marriage, when God brought the man and the woman together to become one flesh as husband and wife (Gen. 2:18–25).

Finally, while it's true that we have no record of Jesus speaking about homosexuality during His earthly sojourn, the Holy Spirit, whom Jesus said He would send to speak His words (John 16:12–14), superintended what Paul wrote, so that he wrote exactly what God desired to be written. Second Timothy 3:16 says, "All Scripture is breathed out by God" (ESV). And Second Peter 1:21 says, "No prophecy was ever produced by the will of man, but men spoke from God as they were carried along by the Holy Spirit" (ESV).

Strictly speaking, then, Jesus did not stop speaking when Matthew, Mark, Luke, and John finished their gospel accounts. While Jesus was still on earth, He told the disciples "I have many more things to say to you, but you cannot bear them now" (John 16:12). But He promised that the Holy Spirit would come to the disciples and would guide them into all truth (16:13). This was a promise from Jesus that the Word the Holy Spirit would speak through the disciples would be Christ's own words. In this way, the Spirit would glorify Jesus, as He said, "For He will take of Mine and will disclose it to you" (16:14).

And the Holy Spirit did just that. As the church was being built, the Spirit spoke Jesus' words to the writers of the New Testament. All Scripture—which, according to Second Peter 3:16, included Paul's writings—is God-breathed. It is the very Word of God Himself.

"But didn't men write Scripture?" Yes, but these passages teach that the Holy Spirit so superintended the minds and wills of the writers that the words they wrote under their own recognizance were precisely what God wanted to say to His people. That's what Peter meant when he said they were "carried along" by the Holy Spirit (2 Pet. 1:21). The book of Acts, all the way through to the book of Revelation, are all filled with the very words of God Himself. And, since God exists eternally as Father, Son, and Spirit, and since Jesus is God the Son, all Scripture is the Word of Christ. All Scripture is the Lord of the church speaking to His church by means of the Holy Spirit through the agency of human writers.

That means Jesus did address homosexuality. He did so by sending His Spirit to superintend the writing of Paul, such that Paul wrote precisely what Jesus intended—so much that it was "God-breathed."

Jesus condemned homosexuality by means of Paul's condemnation of homosexuality. Therefore, to deny that homosexuality is sinful is to deny Jesus' own words, something that is irreconcilable with true, biblical Christianity (Luke 9:26).

Does Love Demand Affirmation?

The fifth argument is perhaps the most widespread. It alleges that the above reasoning has lost the big picture. The centerpiece of Jesus' instruction was to love one another. Therefore, His followers should value love wherever it is found and shouldn't have a problem with two consenting adults making a loving commitment to each other.

"Love is love!" they shout at us, rather unlovingly. Failure to affirm homosexuality is charged to be hateful, not loving, and therefore not consistent with Christianity.

Well, yes, love is love. But love "does not rejoice in unrighteousness, but rejoices with the truth" (1 Cor. 13:6). A culture that revels in unrighteousness and rejects even the existence of truth, therefore, can have absolutely no sound understanding of what love is.

The foolish wisdom of secular society has failed to define love biblically. To our self-indulgent, narcissistic, perennially adolescent, self-willed culture, "love" means nothing more than unconditional positive regard. To love someone, according to our society, is to affirm every decision they make and to applaud them just for being them. And that's understandable. To be affirmed without qualification makes us feel good about ourselves. It's nice to be told that we're amazing, just the way we are.

Because of that, people have confused true love with the idea of being affirmed, accepted, flattered, and made much of. "Loving me means making me feel good by making much of me."

Those who have imbibed that definition of love then turn to the Bible, and they read that God is love (1 John 4:8), that "God so loved the world" (John 3:16), that the greatest commandment in the Law is that you love God and love others (Matt. 22:37–40), and that everyone will know you're Jesus' disciples if you love one another (John 13:35).

But then, rather than surrendering their own preconceptions to the authority of God's Word and seeking to understand how God defines love, they use their own distorted definition of love, which they've inherited from society, and they foist that definition of love onto the Scriptures and onto their conception of God.

Then, when they hear that "God is love," they think, "God doesn't demand that people change. God doesn't judge anyone. God accepts everyone just as he or she is. So, Christians must do the same."

That just isn't true; that is not how God defines love. "In this is love," says First John 4:10, "not that we loved God, but that He loved us and sent His Son to be the propitiation for our sins." Or Romans 5:8: "God demonstrates His own love for us in that while we were yet sinners, Christ died for us." These passages and dozens more teach us that love is acting to secure someone's greatest benefit. They don't teach that God thought we were so wonderful, just the way we were, that He would deliver His Son to death to show us how much He thought of us. No, they teach that God labors, at great cost to Himself, to secure the greatest benefit for His beloved.

What do I mean? When we were dead in our sin, cut off from God, and without hope, what would have been our greatest benefit? A perfectly righteous, wrath-propitiating, sin-bearing substitute. And that is exactly what God gave us. He demonstrated His own love by benefitting us with Himself in the person of His beloved Son. Biblically, love does not mean unconditional acceptance, unqualified affirmation, or never hurting someone's feelings. Biblical love labors to secure the beloved's greatest benefit.

And what is everyone's greatest benefit? Not unconditional affirmation. Some say, "Why not? That feels good!" Because God did not design humans to be satisfied by the glory of self. The vision of your own glory and self-exaltation might feel good for a little while, but it will not satisfy the longings of your soul for eternity. You just haven't been designed that way.

So, the people who seek to satisfy you by making much of you do not love you. They lie to you, and they work to rob you of the true joy and lasting satisfaction that come only from looking away from yourself to the glory of God.

Your Creator designed your soul so that you will be most satisfied by the sight of His glory rather than your own. And He defines spiritual life as the ability to see the light of the knowledge of the glory of God in the face of Christ (2 Cor. 4:6). This means love is helping someone see and know and enjoy God in the person of His Son. That is the greatest benefit you can accomplish for anyone.

Love is not unconditional affirmation. Love is working hard, often even suffering, so those you love might be led away from the worship of themselves to find joy in making much of Christ forever. For the sake of their greatest benefit, love is willing to be mocked, to be falsely accused of hatred and bigotry, and even to say and do what might strain a relationship—all so your loved ones might find lasting satisfaction where they were designed to find it: in Christ alone.

Since all of that is true, it becomes plain that acquiescing to the homosexualist agenda of unconditional affirmation is the opposite of love. In fact, to never warn someone that unrepentant homosexuals will not inherit the kingdom of God is to hate them, not love them. It does not benefit sinners if Christians affirm a lifestyle that, if not repented of, will end in eternal destruction. It is not showing hatred to warn people of that danger. It is showing hatred to fail to issue such warnings.

It would be like watching a friend driving his car toward a cliff he doesn't realize is there. Even if he reported that he was enjoying himself, that driving is fun, and that he can see no danger, it is not loving to affirm and encourage him as he speeds to his destruction. It is loving to alert him of the cliff and steer him to safety.

"Who do you think you are to force your views on him? Can't you see how much he enjoys this? He's not hurting anybody. Just leave him alone and worry about yourself!" The person who reprimands you for doing that does not love the man in the car.

Dear reader, we do not love like Jesus loves if we unconditionally affirm someone in a choice that robs him or her of true, abiding satisfaction and leads him to ruin. We love like Jesus loves when we graciously and patiently proclaim a message that has the power to free people from the bondage of their suicidal love affair with themselves—the power to liberate them into the freedom and the joy of making much of the glory of God.

We love like God loves when we point people away from worshipping themselves and their own desires and when we steer them toward their greatest benefit: God Himself.

Win the Person

So, steer people away from sin, proclaim the gospel of forgiveness in Jesus Christ, and answer these objections when they are raised in response to the gospel—not because we care most about winning an argument, but because we care about winning the person.

When people aim to evade the piercing sword of God's law, they cut themselves off from the healing balm of the gospel. But if you can engage them intelligently, biblically, compassionately, and patiently by answering their sincere objections, perhaps those superficial barriers in their mind will break down.

We can't argue someone out of the bondage of sin or into the kingdom of God. But we pray that God will use these answers to their objections to help them hear the gospel with a fresh openness, and we pray that the Holy Spirit will grant them the new birth, to renew their hearts, to give them eyes to see, and to bring them to repentance, faith, and freedom from sin.

Study Questions:

1. How is marriage a parable of the gospel? What implications does that have for the permissibility of homosexual "marriage"?
2. Some argue that it's wrong to insist on the sinfulness of homosexuality on the basis of Old Testament commands, because Christians disobey commands about eating shellfish and pork. How would you respond to a friend who made that objection?
3. What was the purpose of the ceremonial laws of the Mosaic covenant? What is their relationship to new covenant believers? What passages of Scripture guide your thinking on this?
4. In what ways are the Old Testament commands prohibiting homosexuality different from ceremonial laws regulating diet and clothing?
5. A popular argument says "homosexual" is a mistranslation of the original language, and that Paul did not mean to condemn "loving, committed, monogamous same-sex relationships," but only abusive or pedophilic practices. How would you respond to a friend who made that objection?
6. How would you respond to a friend who asked, "If homosexuality is such a big deal, why didn't Jesus say anything about it?"
7. The chapter claims that "all Scripture is the word of Christ." What is the biblical argument for this claim? What are the implications of that for this discussion?
8. How can you respond to a friend who insists that "love is love," and that it's unloving not to affirm homosexuals?

6

Is Same-Sex Attraction Sinful?

THE PREVIOUS CHAPTER was designed to vindicate the Bible's teaching concerning the sinfulness of homosexual practice. Any sexual activity between members of the same sex is clearly prohibited by Scripture, and arguments to the contrary have proven unconvincing. However, even within conservative evangelicalism, a growing number of people believe that, while homosexual practice is incompatible with faithful Christian profession, homosexual orientation is not necessarily sinful.

While many call same-sex attraction "disordered" or "a product of the fall," they hesitate to say that same-sex desires are sinful in and of themselves. Some say that those who experience sexual desires for or attraction to members of the same sex do not necessarily need to mortify those desires, which, they say, can be spiritually unhealthy. Instead, those who experience same-sex attraction are counseled to redirect those desires in some sort of lawful expression.

This question—the sinfulness or permissibility of same-sex attraction—is a watershed issue for conservative evangelical conviction on sexuality. We understand that the Bible condemns homosexual practice. We understand that it's unwise and contrary to our life in Christ to define ourselves by our sinful inclinations, and so we reject such terminology as "gay Christian." But evangelicals seem to be confused over whether sexual attraction to members of the same sex is sinful in itself or whether it is neutral until acted upon.

The way Bible-believing Christians answer this question will have far-reaching effects—not only on our doctrine of sanctification in general but also on our ability to uphold a consistent biblical sexual ethic in the face of so many hostile opponents in the culture.

The goal of this chapter is to show that same-sex attraction is indeed sin that requires repentance. As a result, pastors and church leaders have a responsibility to help those with same-sex attraction to mortify and forsake those desires. Alternatively, legitimizing same-sex attraction in any sense would be the breach in the dam that would lead to full-scale compromise on biblical sexuality.

Compassionate Concern

Our ultimate concern for this matter rises out of a desire for Jesus Christ to get what He is worthy of in the church He purchased with His blood (Acts 20:28). He gave Himself to redeem His people "from every lawless deed, and to purify for Himself a people for His own possession, zealous for good deeds" (Titus 2:14).

Those who love their Savior want to see His holy standard for sexual ethics upheld amid virulent attacks from a godless culture. The glory of God and lordship of Christ is our ultimate concern.

But we're also driven to discuss this out of compassionate concern for those who struggle with same-sex attraction. We have no desire to place an undue burden on followers of Christ, who, out of obedience to Him, discipline themselves to not engage in homosexual behavior, even though it's what seems most natural to them.

In their helpful book, *Transforming Homosexuality*, Denny Burk and Heath Lambert articulate this concern quite well.

> These dear brothers and sisters struggle faithfully and practice chastity, but they sense that they cannot eliminate same-sex attractions that well up within them spontaneously and uninvited. So it seems cruel and unusual to call their unchosen and unwanted attractions sinful. To call their attractions sinful while they are otherwise living a life of faithfulness and chastity . . . seems to load these brothers and sisters up with burdens too heavy for them to bear. And no one wants to sin against them and fall under the censure that Jesus laid against the scribes and Pharisees.[1]

That's exactly right. Nevertheless, if Scripture prohibits not merely homosexual behavior but also the desires and inclinations that lead to that behavior, then to demonstrate that to our struggling brothers and sisters is not to place an undue burden upon them. It's to make God's will known to them and to bring to bear on their lives Scripture's standard of holiness, a standard that God gives them for their good and blessing.

That is something every follower of Jesus needs his brothers and sisters to do for him. If I'm convinced that I'm not sinning when I actually am, I need my fellow believers to help me see what I'm blind to. Otherwise, I may continue in unrepentant sin and thereby sacrifice the communion with Christ that is only enjoyed on the path of obedience. Such fellowship is hindered when I harbor sin rather than confessing it.

---

1 Denny Burk and Heath Lambert, *Transforming Homosexuality: What the Bible Says about Sexual Orientation and Change* (Phillipsburg, NJ: P&R, 2015), 40.

So, by identifying sin as what it is, our goal is not to place undue burdens on people but to give them hope. It is to say, "Dear brother, you don't have to be enslaved to these sinful desires for the rest of your days. You can find freedom and wholeness in Christ through the sanctifying power of the gospel." His resurrection power is what enables us to walk in newness of life.

Attraction, Desire, and Noticing

With this in mind, it's necessary to define some terms. Someone who is same-sex attracted has enduring experiences of emotional, romantic, and/or sexual desires for members of the same sex. Some who defend the neutrality of same-sex attraction argue that we should distinguish between attraction and desire. One professing Christian teacher contends that after same-sex desires are purified, there remains a "complex set of noticings and attractions toward members of one's own sex."[2] However, the following assessment is a helpful response:

> While noticing is not the same as desire, it is hard to imagine how "attraction" does not carry some sense of magnetic pull, arousal, or desire. By a simple dictionary definition, to notice is to observe or perceive, while attraction suggests interest and allurement. A mother may recognize that her teenage son is quite handsome or that her daughter has grown into an objectively beautiful woman. These noticings can take place apart from any sexual longing. But if a mother were to experience any attraction to her son or daughter, surely we would describe this kind of noticing as illicit, as a perverse response—however unbidden—that should be mortified at all costs. In short, while we distinguish between noticing and attraction, we do not see how attraction and desire are fundamentally different moral categories.[3]

That is well said. To be attracted to someone is to desire that person in some way. To be same-sex attracted is to experience enduring emotional, romantic, and/or sexual desires for members of the same sex. And even if those desires arise subconsciously and are unwanted, they are nevertheless sinful and must be mortified.

But why? Why are homosexual desires and attractions sinful, and why must we counsel those who struggle with such desires and attractions to repent of them?

---

2 This comment comes from a talk given by Matthew Lee Anderson at the Revoice Conference of 2018. It is produced as cited in "Central Carolina Presbytery Study Committee Report on 2018 Revoice Conference," www.ccpca.net/news/ccp_study_committee_report_on_2018_revoice_conference.pdf (accessed December 2023).

3 "Central Carolina Presbytery Study Committee Report," emphasis original.

THE INTERNAL NATURE OF SIN AND HOLINESS

We must counsel those who struggle with such attractions to repent of them because sin and holiness are matters of the heart and cannot be reduced merely to external actions. Genuine, God-honoring, Christlike, Spirit-driven holiness is a matter of a person's thoughts, affections, and desires—not just his or her actions. God does not only command His people to behave righteously, He also commands us to be holy. The believer's growth in holiness is a fundamentally internal matter.[4]

Scripture's emphasis on the heart speaks to our need to forsake sin and pursue holiness in the inner man. In Matthew 5:8, Jesus said, "Blessed are the pure in heart, for they shall see God."

It is not enough to clean the outside of the cup and the dish when inside they are full of robbery and self-indulgence. It's not enough to whitewash the tombs when inside they are full of dead men's bones and all uncleanness. No, Jesus says, "First clean the inside of the cup and of the dish, so that the outside of it may also become clean" (Matt. 23:26). Jesus taught that the Father is not satisfied with hypocritical forgiveness, but will cast us into hell to be tortured "if each of you does not forgive his brother from your heart" (Matt. 18:35).

The greatest commandment in the law, Matthew 22:37, is that we love the Lord our God with all our heart, with all our soul, and with all our mind. When Simon the sorcerer sought to buy the gift of the Holy Spirit, Peter called him to repent, and to pray "that, if possible, the intention of your heart may be forgiven you" (Acts 8:22).

When the gospel releases us from our slavery to sin, Paul said believers "became obedient from the heart to that form of teaching to which you were committed" (Rom. 6:17). Elsewhere, he commanded slaves to be obedient to their masters "in the sincerity of your heart, as to Christ; not by way of eyeservice, as men-pleasers, but as slaves of Christ, doing the will of God from the heart" (Eph. 6:5–6).

And in progressive sanctification, God works in us not just to work, but also to will—even on our desires (Phil. 2:12–13). This means the desires of our flesh, which characterized our old life of sin, are to be the object of our mortification. The New Testament also testifies to that. Paul said that the passions and the desires of the flesh must be crucified in those who belong to Christ Jesus (Gal. 5:24).

God's grace instructs us to deny ungodliness and worldly desires (Titus 2:11–12). Peter urged believers to abstain from fleshly desires that wage war against the

4 Portions of this section are adapted from Michael Riccardi, *Sanctification: The Christian's Pursuit of God-Given Holiness* (Sun Valley, CA: Grace Books, 2015).

soul (1 Pet. 2:11). And Colossians 3:5 says we are to put to death what is earthly in us—not merely the external actions of "sexual immorality and impurity," but also the internal affections of "passion, evil desire, and covetousness" (ESV).

These texts testify that Christian holiness is not merely a matter of conforming our outward behavior to an external standard. Charles Hodge likens the work of sanctification to "making the tree good, in order that the fruit may be good."[5] You don't staple fruit to a tree; you ground the roots of the tree in the richness of the soil, whose nutrients produce life. Hodge notes, "Sanctification in its essential nature is not holy acts, but such a change in the state of the soul, that sinful acts become more infrequent, and holy acts more and more habitual and controlling."[6]

Therefore, sanctification is both internal and external. We must have sanctified affections as well as sanctified actions—because God has not simply commanded us to carry out a series of external duties. He has also commanded us to have a particular frame of heart as we do those external duties. We are not merely to do justly but to love mercy (Mic. 6:8). Pastors and elders are to shepherd the flock of God willingly and eagerly, not under compulsion (1 Pet. 5:2). Christians have a duty to worship God through giving, but God loves a cheerful giver (2 Cor. 9:7). If you give your offering every week, but do it begrudgingly, you may have done your external duty to give, but you have not done your internal duty of giving cheerfully.

The point is that God commands our affections as well as our actions. The truly holy person doesn't only follow a to-do list of external commands; he loves and desires what God desires. He is attracted to the things that God is attracted to and acts in keeping with that renewed heart.

Heart and Hands, Root and Fruit

The notion, then, that a person faithfully follows Christ as long as he doesn't act on his corrupt desires is out of accord with Scripture's doctrine of sanctification. To suggest that a Christian man may lawfully entertain emotional, romantic, or sexual desires for another man—as long as he doesn't act on them—is to cut the heart out of biblical holiness.

Rather than making the tree good, as Hodge says, it is nothing more than chopping off the rotten fruit, while allowing (and in some cases even

5 Charles Hodge, *Systematic Theology*, 3 vols. (Grand Rapids: Eerdmans, 1968), 3:226.

6 Hodge, *Systematic Theology*, 3:226.

encouraging) sin to continue to draw life from the soil of corruption. But we are not to battle sin merely at the level of its fruit. We are to lay the axe at the root of the tree. Jesus taught that sinful acts are rooted in, and grow out of, our sinful hearts (Mark 7:21). Our affections and desires produce the very behaviors that must be mortified. This means those affections and desires also must be put off.

Jesus addressed this in the Sermon on the Mount. In Matthew 5:27, He quoted from the Greek translation of the seventh commandment that was given in Exodus 20:14: "You have heard that it was said, 'YOU SHALL NOT COMMIT ADULTERY.'" That is a prohibition of sexually immoral behavior. But then, in verse 28, He immediately followed this with a citation of the tenth commandment, a prohibition of sexually immoral desire: "But I say to you that everyone who looks at a woman with lust for her"—literally, "to desire her"—"has already committed adultery with her in his heart."

The term translated "lust" is *epithumeō*, from the Greek translation of Exodus 20:17, "You shall not covet [*epithumeō*] your neighbor's wife." Jesus inextricably linked the pre-behavioral sexual desire for a woman with the sinful act of adultery.[7] God's law doesn't merely prohibit acts of adultery and stealing; it prohibits the covetous and lustful desires that lead to those acts.

Therefore, to divorce same-sex desires from same-sex behavior, and to suggest that the latter is prohibited while the former is permissible, is to externalize the concepts of sin and holiness. This undermines the biblical doctrine of sanctification to make way for mere behavior modification.[8] This would leave us hypocritically forcing ourselves to abstain from what our hearts long for, rather than causing us to be transformed from the inside out by the power of the gospel.

Sin is not merely what we do or even what we feel. Outside of Christ, sin is who we are. It is not simply our transgression of external laws, but the condition of our souls.

The fact that sinful desires seem to spring from within us so naturally does not make our desires less sinful. That we seem naturally oriented towards or attracted to a particular set of sinful behaviors does not absolve us from culpability; it increases our culpability. The fact that I find temptation to sin to be so enticing only means my sin problem is worse than I thought. It reaches deeper than my hands and into my heart—into the core of who I am. And since my sinful acts are rooted in and spring out from my sinful

7 Burk and Lambert, *Transforming Homosexuality*, 45.

8 Burk and Lambert, *Transforming Homosexuality*, 79.

heart, biblical sanctification requires more than repentance at the level of my behavior; it requires repentance at the level of the desires and the inclinations and the attractions that produce those behaviors.

Longtime professor of theology John Murray put it this way: "The outward act of transgression . . . [is] determined by inclination, propension, character. . . . The character that produce[s] the act cannot be different as to its moral character from the act itself."[9] In other words, it is sin to be attracted to what is sinful. The desire for what God prohibits is itself a prohibited desire. It is an indication that whatever my actions may be, my affections are still sinful. I still want something that my Father has told me is not for me to have.

I may know it's wrong to act on that desire, and by God's grace, I may restrain myself from acting upon it. For instance, it's better to not compound the internal disobedience of lust with the external disobedience of committing adultery. But it still means I want something—I'm still attracted to something—that does not show me more of my God, that does not lead me to enjoy more of His glory, and therefore, cannot satisfy the longings of my soul, but can only deceive (Eph. 4:22), corrupt (2 Pet. 2:10), and plunge me into ruin and destruction (1 Tim. 6:9).

To seek satisfaction in things that are not my God, nor from my God, is evil desire. It is idolatry. It is sin, and I must repent of it.

Is It a Sin to Be Tempted?

If what I've argued above is correct, then same-sex attraction of itself is sin. However, people often object by saying that experiencing same-sex attraction is virtually identical to temptation. To be attracted to sin is to be tempted to sin. And temptation in itself cannot be sinful, because the Lord Jesus "has been tempted in all things as we are, yet without sin" (Heb. 4:15).

If I say that same-sex attraction is sinful, aren't I saying that people sin simply by being tempted? And if so, do I not undermine the sinlessness of Christ, who was tempted?

Internal vs. External Temptation

This is an important objection, one that stands at the very crux of the debate. Ultimately, though this objection conflates two kinds of temptation—or, at least, two ways the Scriptures speak about temptation. We might call them external temptation and internal temptation.

9 John Murray, "The Fall of Man," in *Collected Writings of John Murray, Volume 2: Systematic Theology* (Carlisle, PA: Banner of Truth, 2009), 69.

External temptation is experienced entirely from the outside. It is an external solicitation to sin. Jesus experienced external temptation in the wilderness, when Satan tempted Him to turn stones into bread, to fall down and worship Satan, and to throw Himself from the cliff to prove He was the Son of God (Matt. 4:1–11; Luke 4:1–13). It was not sin for Jesus to be tempted in this way, to be the object of Satan's unsuccessful temptations.

For example, if someone comes to me and says, "Look at that girl! She barely has anything on!" that person, external to me, is tempting me to sin. But if such a temptation finds no place in my affections; if there are no "hooks" in my heart that dispose me to yield to that temptation; if, by God's grace, I was so satisfied in the communion with Christ that I enjoy on the path of obedience that the path of disobedience looks utterly repulsive to me and has no pull on my affections; and if my delight in the glory of the Lord is such that this kind of temptation is lost on me, then I have not sinned. It is not sinful in itself to be tempted externally.

On the other hand, internal temptation is what James describes when he says, "But each one is tempted when he is carried away and enticed by his own lust," or his own desire (James 1:14). Internal temptation arises from within my own sinful heart. It shows that my affections, desires, inclinations, and attractions are still corrupt; I want something my Father has not given to me, something that does not lead me to enjoy His glory in greater measure, and therefore, cannot satisfy my soul. To desire those things that exchange the truth of God for a lie is to commit idolatry.

To use the same scenario, then, if someone urges me to look at an immodestly dressed woman, and if that external temptation combines with my own evil desires to gratify the lust of my eyes, then even if I don't ultimately turn and look, I have still sinned in my heart. I have still desired something for which there is no lawful expression—something the Lord has told me is not mine to have. Therefore, I must repent of that desire and mortify it such that if I were presented with that kind of external temptation again, my heart would have no "hooks" for that temptation.

So, the reason it was not sin for Jesus to be tempted in the wilderness was not merely because He never performed the acts Satan urged. It was because Christ never even desired to perform them. Satan's external temptation never passed into internal temptation in Jesus' heart. Because Jesus was sinless—because He had no sin nature; because "the ruler of this world . . . has nothing in" Him (John 14:30)—there was nothing in His sinless nature that could have produced even a desire for evil.

That means that any temptations Jesus faced were external temptations. If there were any "hooks" in Jesus' heart onto which sin could latch, He would have desired what His Father said was not for Him to have. If in the wilderness He thought, "Oh, I would so love to demonstrate My power and glory as the eternal Son apart from My Father's plan!" He would have become a transgressor. He would not have loved God with all His heart, soul, mind, and strength.

In fallen human beings, the Spirit sets His desire against the flesh (Gal. 5:17). A war is being waged within our members (Rom. 7:23). But Jesus, who came in the likeness of sinful flesh (Rom. 8:3), had no genuinely sinful flesh; there was no internal war. He not only performed righteousness; He loved and desired righteousness at every moment. He never desired to do anything but the will of His Father (John 4:34; 5:19).

Christ was holy in His affections as well as His actions. To not be so would have undermined His sinlessness. As John Owen said, "There is something in . . . our temptations more than was in the temptation of Christ. There is something in ourselves to take part with every temptation; and there is enough in ourselves to tempt us, though nothing else should appear against us. With Christ it was not so, John 14:30."[10]

In All Things Like We Are?

But how does that square with the fact that Jesus "has been tempted in all things as we are, yet without sin?" Doesn't that mean that He would have had to experience the temptation to same-sex attraction?

No, Hebrews 4:15 does not mean that Jesus experienced each temptation—inducements from without and enticements from within—that every human has ever faced.

For instance, He was never tempted with the temptations that are peculiar to being a husband or a father, since He never married or fathered children. Since He died and was glorified in His early 30s, He was never tempted with those temptations that are specific to growing old; for example, temptations that might be associated with forbearing arthritis or dementia. Nor did He ever face those temptations that are peculiar to being a woman, such as enduring the physical pains of childbirth or the emotional trials of hormonal issues.

Such an interpretation also fails exegetically. The phrase "in all things" in Hebrews 4:15 should not be interpreted in an absolutely universal

10 John Owen, *Communion with the Triune God*, in *The Works of John Owen*, 23 vols. (Carlisle, PA: Banner of Truth, 2009), 2:143.

sense. The phrase is used only one other time in Hebrews (2:17–18), where the author also discussed Jesus' temptations. There, he said that Jesus "had to be made like His brethren in all things, so that He might become a merciful and faithful high priest in things pertaining to God, to make propitiation for the sins of the people." In 2:17, there isn't even a qualifying limitation like there is in 4:15: "yet without sin." Nevertheless, it's evident that "in all things" cannot be interpreted in an absolutely universal sense. Jesus was not made like His brethren in absolutely all things without exception. His brethren were sinners; He was not. His brethren were born according to natural generation; He was conceived by the Holy Spirit in the virgin's womb.

When we read Hebrews 2:17, we don't force a wooden universality upon the expression "in all things." No, we understand the author's point: Jesus had to be made like His brethren in all things that required Him to be a suitable substitutionary sacrifice on our behalf. But for the same reason that He had to share our humanity—that is, to be our Mediator—He could not share our sinfulness. Our reading of "in all things" is thus tempered by the context as well as Scripture's unified insistence upon the sinlessness of Christ.

The same should be the case for our reading of "in all things" in 4:15—and even more since there is the qualifying phrase, "yet without sin." Jesus was tempted without sin. This does not merely mean Jesus was tempted with the result that He never sinned. It also means that sin was never the principle of His temptations. Sinful people like us are often tempted by the sin that lives within us.

External temptations combine with the indwelling sin of our flesh to induce us to perform outward acts of wickedness. James meant this when he said, "Each one is tempted when he is carried away and enticed by his own lust" (James 1:14). But Jesus could never have been tempted in that way, because He had no indwelling sin to cooperate with external allurements.

According to the Likeness

This is at least one way Jesus' temptations are different from ours. It is an example of what it means for His temptations to be "according to the likeness" of ours. That's actually the literal translation of the phrase, "as we are."

He was tempted in all things according to the likeness of our temptations. But His temptations were "without sin," and so they were unlike ours in that way. John Owen explains this with great insight:

> He was also like unto us in temptations, for the reason which the apostle gives in the last verse. But herein also some difference may be observed between him and us; for the most of our temptations arise from within us, from our own unbelief and lusts. Again, in those that are from without [i.e., external temptations], there is some[thing] in us to take part with them, which always makes us fail in our duty of resistance, and ofttimes leads to further miscarriages. But from these things he was absolutely free; for as he had no inward disposition or inclination unto the least evil [i.e., internal temptations], being perfect in all graces and all their operations at all times, so when the prince of this world came unto him, he had no part in him [John 14:30],—nothing to close with his suggestions or to entertain his terrors.[11]

Elsewhere, Owen comments on the phrase "without sin." He writes, "And hereby the apostle preserves in us due apprehensions of the purity and holiness of Christ, that we may not imagine that he was liable unto any such temptations unto sin from within [internal temptations] as we find ourselves liable unto, which are never free from guilt and defilement."[12]

So, Jesus was tempted by all kinds of temptations common to humans, in a manner similar to us, yet without sin, and so never in such a way that His temptations arose from within. He was tempted externally, like we are; yet without sin, and thus He was not tempted internally.

Owen explains this distinction between internal and external temptation very well in his work on indwelling sin:

> Now, what is it to be tempted? It is to have that proposed to a man's consideration which, if he close withal, it is evil, it is sin unto him. This is sin's trade: *Epithumei*—"It lusteth." It is raising up in the heart, and proposing unto the mind and affections, that which is evil; trying, as it were, whether the soul will close with its suggestions, or how far it will carry them on, though it do not wholly prevail. Now, when such a temptation comes from without, it is unto the soul an indifferent thing, neither good nor evil, unless it be consented unto; but the very proposal from within, it being the soul's own act, is its sin.[13]

The proposal of temptation from within the heart of man is the soul's own act, and therefore it is sin. The "temptation" of same-sex attraction is an

11 John Owen, *The Epistle to the Hebrews*, in *The Works of John Owen*, 23 vols. (Carlisle, PA: Banner of Truth Trust, 2009), 19:468.

12 John Owen, *The Epistle to the Hebrews*, 20:427.

13 John Owen, *The Nature and Power of Indwelling Sin*, in *The Works of John Owen*, 23 vols. (Carlisle, PA: Banner of Truth, 2009), 6:194.

internal temptation. It is to be carried away and enticed by a person's own desire, and therefore it is sin.

DESIRE, SIN, AND JAMES 1:13–15

Another oft-raised objection concerns the progression of thought in James 1:13–15. Didn't James distinguish sin from desire in that text? James wrote, "Each one is tempted when he is carried away and enticed by his own lust," or desire. "Then when [desire] has conceived, it gives birth to sin; and when sin is accomplished, it brings forth death." I've argued that the desire for sin is sin, but here James said the desire leads to sin. Does this put me at odds with the apostle James?

No—because of the distinct ways the New Testament uses the term "sin" (Gk. *hamartia*). Some texts use the term to refer to particular sinful deeds or behaviors. The Prodigal Son came to his father and said, "Father, I have sinned" (Luke 15:18). Or, "I have committed deeds of iniquity."

In other texts, sin refers to that condition of sin that plagues the soul—the inclination to sin in the fallen human heart. This is that "law of sin" in the members of my body that wages war against the "law of my mind" (Rom 7:23). So "sin" can be used to speak of individual acts of sin or sin as a principle that dwells in sinners.

Interestingly, of the seven times James used the word *hamartia* in his letter, every other occurrence was a clear reference to sinful deeds: "But if you show partiality, you are committing sin" (2:9); "Confess your sins to one another" (5:16; 4:17; 5:15, 20).

Given James's usage of the word in the rest of the letter, along with the New Testament's teaching on the fundamentally internal nature of sin and holiness, we are constrained to interpret "sin" in James 1:15 to refer to the commission of sinful acts.[14] In this verse, James spoke of sin as the actual external act of sin. He did not mean to define sin as wholly external and not at all internal. That would contradict the above passages concerning the fundamentally internal nature of sin and holiness.

Calvin agreed with this interpretation of James 1. In his commentary, he explicitly distinguished his view from the Roman Catholic doctrine of concupiscence.

> It seems, however, improper, and not according to the usage of Scripture, to restrict the word sin to outward works, as though indeed lust

14 Burk and Lambert, *Transforming Homosexuality*, 54.

> itself were not a sin, and as though corrupt desires, remaining closed up within and suppressed, were not so many sins. But as the use of a word is various, there is nothing unreasonable if it be taken here, as in many other places, for actual sin [that is, the commission of external acts of sin]. And the Papists ignorantly lay hold on this passage, and seek to prove from it that vicious, yea, filthy, wicked, and the most abominable lusts are not sins, provided there is no assent; for James does not shew when sin begins to be born, so as to be sin, and so accounted by God, but when it breaks forth.[15]

Calvin was right: James wasn't telling us when sin begins, but when sin breaks forth. The Central Carolina Presbytery provides a helpful amplification of Calvin's commentary.

> For Calvin, there is indwelling sin (the temptations caused by desire in v. 14b), actual sin (the birth of sin in v. 15a), and . . . "perfected" sin (the deadly fully grown sin in v. 15b). When James talks about temptations leading to sin, he does not mean that the temptation (in this case) is itself morally neutral. . . . The one who is experiencing temptation caused by his own desire (*epithumias*) is already experiencing the reality of indwelling sin, though that indwelling sin (in the Christian) can be resisted so as not to give birth to actual (i.e., acted upon) sin. . . . [The] process [outlined in James 1:14–15] is not one that moves from innocence to sin, but rather one that sees indwelling sin move from the mind to the affections to the will and finally to the outward working of sin in the life (and death) of a person.[16]

In other words, James's point was simple: Sinful desire gives birth to sinful acts. But it doesn't follow from that to conclude that the "desire" he speaks about is morally neutral. The text says such desire lures and entices the sinner away from faithfulness and into disobedience. That's why several translations render *epithumia* as "lust," here: It's plain from the context that this desire has a sinful character. While the objection from James 1 seems plausible at first, not only does it fail to establish the neutrality of desire; upon closer examination, it actually establishes the sinfulness of desire.

In fact, that's what covetousness is: a desire for anything you cannot righteously have—a desire for which there is no lawful expression. Sexual attraction to members of the same sex fits that definition precisely.

---

15 John Calvin, *Commentaries on the Catholic Epistles*, in vol. 22 of *Calvin's Commentaries*, trans. John Owen (Grand Rapids: Baker Books, 2009), 290.

16 "Central Carolina Presbytery Study Committee Report," 8–9.

Some object, "It's not a sin for a man to find a woman attractive, as long as it doesn't pass into lustful desire. Why can't it be the same for a man finding men attractive?"

Well, first, same-sex attraction goes beyond noticing that someone is objectively pleasant-looking. Second, heterosexual desire and homosexual desire are just different things. The morality of a desire is determined by its object. It's not a matter of intensity—"I like it, but only a little bit"—or a matter of chosenness—"Yes, I confess I want it, but I really don't want to want it." It's a matter of the thing desired. The object of heterosexual desire may be lawfully expressed within the covenant of marriage. But the object of homosexual desire cannot be lawfully expressed. And a desire for which there is no lawful expression is the definition of covetousness. It is the very evil desire that Colossians 3:5 commands us to regard as dead to us, and that Colossians 3:6 says brings about the wrath of God upon unbelievers.

Reorienting Freedom

I am not saying that a person who struggles with same-sex attraction must not be a Christian. But he or she must be exhorted to put off sinful affections—just like someone who is particularly susceptible to the temptations of fornication, or adultery, or drunkenness, or acts of violence.

A colleague once told me about a man who wrote to the colleague's ministry in search of encouragement. "He wanted us to agree with his belief that mere attraction to a forbidden object is not inherently sinful," he said. The man gave a credible testimony of salvation and reported that he actively served in his church. Finally, he revealed that he felt a sexual attraction to "large farm animals."

How should a Christian counsel that man? Or what about the man who, for as long as he can remember, has been marked by an unwanted attraction to young children? Should we tell him that his attractions are morally neutral, as long as he doesn't act on his desires? No, we should tell these people to put those evil desires to death, because those desires are themselves sinful.

What about Christians who struggle with anger to the point that they are tempted to physically harm others? We don't teach "violence-attracted Christians" to make peace with their "orientation." We teach them to confess such inclinations and attractions as sinful, to put them to death by the Spirit, and to walk in accordance with the gospel by which they profess to be saved.

Those who deny the sinfulness of same-sex attraction do not give hope to those who struggle with it. In that perspective, there is no hope for freedom from the bondage of unwanted desires. Instead of helping struggling believers overcome sin, this perspective lies to them and seeks to define the problem away. But those who confess the sinfulness of same-sex attraction have so much better news than, "You're stuck. You're going to have to learn to manage these disordered affections for as long as you live." We have the gospel of sovereign grace that brings genuine reorienting freedom in Christ.

Yes, we are constrained by Scripture to confess that same-sex attraction is itself sinful. But we are constrained by the same Scriptures to declare that Christ Jesus has come into the world to save sinners (1 Tim. 1:15). And He came not only to justify sinners on the basis of His own perfect obedience (Phil. 3:9), but also to sanctify them by the exertion of the same power that raised Him from the dead (Phil. 3:10). Resurrection power is at work for the sanctification of those who trust in Christ (Rom. 6:4).

It would be unwise to promise or expect immediate change. Christ doesn't often immediately banish any trace of temptation with any long-cherished sinful desire. Nevertheless, we do have the great hope that so-called sexual orientation is not immutable. Many believers have labored diligently to put same-sex attraction to death, and many have reported victory.

Our sexuality is an aspect of our lives over which Christ our King asserts His Lordship, and we must trust Him to do far more abundantly beyond all that we can ask or think through the means of grace that He has appointed for our sanctification.

Christ Our Champion

Beyond all this, we each should worship Jesus Christ—the Captain of our salvation, our Champion of perfect righteousness—who never sinned by having any sinful sexual desires. He was truly human, like us, tempted like we are and yet without sin—without sin in hand or in heart, but perfectly pure.

Dear Christian, your Lord walked as a man on this earth, and He never took advantage of anyone with a lustful glance. He never viewed others as an occasion for His own gratification. He always interacted with His neighbors in perfect purity. He always lived for their benefit, and never once sought to use anyone for His own illicit gain.

What a Man! What a Savior! Whether we struggle with same-sex attraction or any other sin, the cry of our hearts should be, "Dear Father, make me like the Lord Jesus."

And, praise God, where we have failed, He has succeeded. Where you have sinned, dear reader, He has obeyed. And He freely credits that real-life, lived-out, perfect life of obedience to all who come to Him in faith.

Such a contemplation of His glory transforms us into the same image (2 Cor. 3:18). Therefore, let us look to Him. Let us run with endurance, fixing our eyes on Jesus (Heb. 12:1–2). And let us point others to Him as well—especially those who struggle with same-sex attraction—so that Christ may cleanse them through faith and purify them for His own possession.

He is worthy of a pure bride, inside and out. And He stands ready to dispense that grace for His glory and our joy.

Study Questions:

1. Why is it more compassionate to insist on the sinfulness of same-sex attraction?
2. What are the differences between noticing, desire, and attraction? What bearing does that have on the sinfulness of same-sex attraction?
3. What are some key passages of Scripture that focus on the internal nature of sin and holiness?
4. In light of passages like Micah 6:8, Second Corinthians 9:7, and First Peter 5:2, can you truly obey God even if you don't "feel like it"?
5. Why is it not unfair for God to command our emotions?
6. What's the difference between internal temptation and external temptation? Is it necessarily sin to be tempted externally? Is it necessarily sin to be tempted internally?
7. Does Hebrews 4:15 mean that Jesus experienced every single human temptation possible? Why or why not?
8. Why does James 1:13–15 not exclude evil desire from being sinful?
9. What determines the morality of a desire? What does not determine the morality of a desire? Support your answers with Scripture.

7

Loving Leadership

The Biblical Man as Leader and Lover

IN THE PREVIOUS chapters, we established that men and women are different by the holy and wise design of God. They are alike in their humanity, unified as equal image-bearers of God, but distinct in their gender, complementing each other as a harmony of praise to the God who created them. As a result, we concluded that men glorify God when they act like men, and women glorify God when they act like women.

But what does it mean, according to Scripture, to behave like a man, or like a woman? Aside from the obvious biological differences, what does it mean to be a biblical man and not a woman? What does it mean to be a biblical woman and not a man?[1]

If there is glory in our distinctiveness, it's fitting to devote ourselves to understand the beauty of those distinctions, above all so we can order our lives according to the Bible's prescriptions and thereby bring honor and glory to God.

Masculine Men for the Benefit of Women

Women never flourish more than when men act like men. The greatest thing that could happen to the women of Christ's church is for the men of the church to live out their calling as men in ways that line up with the biblical standard.

But that truth is secular heresy in our culture. The accepted thinking of our world today is that masculinity is toxic, a relic of outmoded patriarchal societies, which has resulted in the subjugation and abuse of women.

1 John Piper, *What's the Difference?: Manhood and Womanhood Defined according to the Bible* (Wheaton: Crossway, 1990), 17.

Rather than calling men to be manly, the wisdom of the age calls men to think, speak, and act as little like men as possible.

Now, certainly abuses have occurred. Rather than the biblical pattern of loving, servant-hearted, sacrificial headship, the world has perverted the good gift of male headship into cruel, heavy handed domination. And that is sin. It is wickedness to repent of and forsake.

But the answer to those abuses is not to so stress the truth of men's and women's equality that our distinctiveness is minimized. The answer to misogyny is not misandry. The answer to men's mistreatment of women is not to mistreat men. The answer to injustice is not to perpetrate more injustice—only in the opposite direction. It is not to condemn masculinity as inherently toxic and seek to eradicate healthy expressions of it.

Feminism's attempts to emasculate society have produced no genderless utopia. Instead, the deprecation of gender distinctiveness has given us a culture of males who don't know how to be men and females who don't know how to be women. John Piper rightly observed,

> The consequence of this confusion is not a free and happy harmony among gender-free persons relating on the basis of abstract competencies. The consequence is rather more divorce, more homosexuality, more sexual abuse, more promiscuity, more social awkwardness, and more emotional distress and suicide that come with the loss of God-given identity.[2]

The chaos of the present moment illustrates that the deprecation of masculinity and femininity does not result in blessing, because it is rebellion against God's good design. God has designed that He receive glory and that women flourish most when men act like men.

SINGLENESS AND MARRIAGE

We need to make the observation that marriage is the norm for God's image-bearers. Immediately after God made man male and female (Gen. 1:27), He commanded them to procreate (Gen. 1:28). Immediately after woman was discovered as man's suitable helper (Gen. 2:22–23), we witness the first marriage (Gen. 2:24).

Though the Lord does not grant everyone the gift of marriage, it is nevertheless the norm for ordering society, and therefore much of Scripture's teaching on masculinity and femininity applies to marriage or preparing for marriage.

---

2 Piper, *What's the Difference?* 16–17.

Still, we should not tie manhood and womanhood exclusively to marriage. You are not less of a man or a woman if you're not married. The most biblical man in the history of the world was single. Jesus of Nazareth never married, never had sexual relations, never raised His own biological children, and He was the holiest, happiest, most fulfilled person who ever walked the earth.

The greatest missionary in history, the apostle Paul, labored for the glory of God and the propagation of the gospel without taking along a wife (1 Cor. 9:5). If you are single, you are at no disadvantage to living out the calling of your manhood—not any more than Jesus or Paul were. There are biblical, appropriate expressions of masculinity from single men, even toward the women in your life who are not your wife. The instruction that follows will seek to make application to both married and single men.

Man is a Leader

The first mark of biblical manhood to consider is that a man is a leader. When Paul said, "The husband is the head of the wife, as Christ also is the head of the church" (Eph. 5:23), he identified the husband as the head, or the leader, of his family. Paul elsewhere spoke more broadly than the husband-wife relationship and said, "But I want you to understand that Christ is the head of every man, and the man is the head of a woman" (1 Cor. 11:3). Attempts to subvert the plain meaning of these texts ultimately prove unconvincing.

Rooted in Creation

But more than these passages, the truth of male headship is found in the opening chapters of Genesis, concurrent with man's creation. This is significant, because it means that the roles of male headship and female submission are not incidental, later additions to male and female identity.

Even more importantly, these complementary roles for men and women do not have their origin in the fall, when sin corrupted our relationships with one another. The biblical complementarity of male headship and female submission are not rooted in culture or corruption but in creation. The early chapters of Genesis bear this out in several ways.

First, God created the man first (Gen. 2:7). You might ask, "Is being created first an indication of headship?" The apostle Paul thought so, because he interpreted it as a ground for the man's leadership role in the church. In First Timothy 2:12–13, he wrote, "But I do not allow a woman to teach or exercise authority over a man, but to remain quiet. *For* it was Adam who was first created, and then Eve." That God made Adam first, Paul noted, was an indication of giving him a leadership role.

Second, God gave His command to Adam (Gen. 2:15–17), before the woman was created (Gen. 2:18). This means God entrusted Adam with the responsibility to teach Eve the words of God, and not vice versa.[3] Eve didn't receive her own set of instructions from God; she received the words of God's law through her head, Adam.

Third, God created the woman from the man. He put Adam into a deep sleep, took his rib, and fashioned the rib into a woman (Gen. 2:21–22). In First Corinthians 11, Paul said, "The woman is the glory of man" (11:7), because "man does not originate from woman, but woman from man" (11:8). This does not make man superior to woman, but it does point to a hierarchy in function. The man's leadership role is grounded in the fact that woman comes from man rather than the other way around.[4]

Fourth, God created the woman *for* the man: "For indeed man was not created for the woman's sake, but woman for the man's sake" (11:9). This refers to God's design in creating the woman to help the man (Gen. 2:18) carry out the divine mandate to "be fruitful and multiply, and fill the earth" (Gen. 1:28). What it means to be woman, in part, is to be one who can suitably help a man walk in obedience to God's commands.

Fifth, the man's headship is seen in the fact that Adam named the woman (Gen. 2:23). Just as Adam named each of the animals (Gen. 2:19), and just as God named His creation throughout Genesis 1, Adam's naming the woman showed authority. A monarch would rename a person to show his own greatness and authority (Gen. 41:45; 2 Kings 23:34; Dan. 1:7). One commentator observed that Eve "found her own identity in relation to the man as his equal and helper *by the man's definition*."[5]

Sixth, with respect to marriage, the man was tasked with the responsibility of initiating a new family: "For this reason a man shall leave his father

---

3 Beeke and Smalley, *Reformed Systematic Theology*, 2:212.

4 That does not mean that man is independent of woman (1 Cor. 11:11), because "as the woman originates from the man, so also the man has his birth through the woman" (11:12). Let us be careful not to distort God's design into ugly one-upmanship. There is distinction of roles, but beautiful interdependence.

5 Raymond C. Ortlund, Jr., "Male-Female Equality and Male Headship: Genesis 1–3," in *Recovering Biblical Manhood and Womanhood: A Response to Evangelical Feminism*, eds. John Piper and Wayne Grudem (Wheaton: Crossway, 2006), 103, emphasis original.

and his mother, and be joined to his wife" (Gen. 2:24). A reader might have expected the passage to say that the woman is to leave her family and be joined to her husband—after all, the woman usually sheds her last name and takes her husband's family name.

However, the man has the responsibility as the head of the household to take the initiative to form the new household.[6] All of these truths testify that leadership is fundamental to the identity of man from the very beginning of his existence.

Leadership as Responsibility

This leadership is not license to do whatever a man pleases. At the heart of biblical, masculine leadership is the concept of responsibility. It's true that the leader is in charge, but Scripture's emphasis isn't as much on the leader's right to govern as he sees fit as much as it is on the leader's stewardship to lead in a way that honors God and benefits those under his charge.

This is also substantiated in the early chapters of Genesis. In the account of the fall of man, Eve was the one who sinned first (3:6). Nevertheless, God called the man to account for the broken commandment (3:9).

As the leader, the man bears the burden of primary accountability for the spiritual and moral health of the family. Creation is cursed because of Adam, not Eve (3:17). Romans 5:12 says that sin entered the world through one man, not one woman. First Corinthians 15:22 says, "In Adam all die." Adam was the head of the human race, and as the head, he bore the responsibility for the spiritual condition of his family.

Masculine leadership, then, means taking responsibility. It means being willing to be held accountable for those under your charge, even when you, personally, may not be at fault. If something is spiritually amiss in your household, men, you bear the ultimate responsibility for that, because God has made you head. This means nothing is less manly than passively abdicating your leadership role and shirking responsibility.

In fact, Adam's transgression consisted in that very passivity—that very abdication of headship and shirking of responsibility. He was responsible to lead his wife, to teach her to obey God's Word, and to protect her against temptation. But he failed to do all these things.

Satan knew that was his way in. He came to the woman first, inverting the God-ordained design of headship and submission, and asked "Indeed, has God said, 'You [plural] shall not eat from any tree of the garden'?" (Gen. 3:1).

6 Ortlund, "Male-Female Equality and Male Headship," 103.

Eve answered, "We may eat" (Gen. 3:2).

Satan made Eve the spokesperson and representative of the family, an office that properly belonged to Adam. This was an immediate, subtle subversion of the very-good, created order of God, defined in the loving headship and sweet submission of man and woman in marriage.

At the point of that temptation, Adam should have been aware of what was going on. He should have stepped in between his wife and the serpent and said, "That's the word He spoke to *me*, snake! You leave her out of this!" And if he tried beguiling her with his crafty speech about becoming like God, knowing good and evil, Adam should have exercised dominion over the creeping thing (Gen. 1:26) and crushed the serpent's head with the heel of his foot.

But he did no such thing. He sat, passively, while his wife was vulnerable and unprotected from the spiritual temptation of the mortal enemy of their souls. He shirked his responsibility to lead her and protect her. Then, he submitted to her sinful leadership, followed her example of disobedience, and ate the fruit God commanded him not to eat.

See how sin and death entered the world by a reversal of God's very-good design for the world! The creeping thing that creeped on the earth ruled over humankind, and the woman exercised headship over the man.[7] All sin traces its origin to the first man's abdication of leadership.

Leadership in Action

If you are going to be a biblical man, you must be a leader. You must be one who takes responsibility, who eschews passivity, who takes action and initiative, who makes decisions with clarity and conviction, and who confronts conflict with boldness and grace.

John Piper wrote, "Mature masculinity . . . feels the responsibility to provide a general pattern of initiative."[8] Especially in the marriage relationship, wives should not feel the burden of primary responsibility to make the household run, while husbands passively respond to her initiative. Men must be imaginative and reflective, thinking about what needs to be done for the family to thrive.

You need to pray at mealtimes, to gather the family for Bible reading and prayer, and to get the family out of bed on Sunday morning so that

7 Owen Strachan and Gavin Peacock, *The Grand Design: Male and Female He Made Them* (Ross-shire, UK: Christian Focus, 2016), 39.

8 Piper, *What's the Difference?*, 31.

everyone gets to church on time. You need to think strategically about how to lead your wife spiritually. What topic of biblical instruction would be beneficial for her spiritual growth at the present moment? What encouragement needs to be given? What correction needs to be given?

You need to think strategically about how to pursue your wife romantically, thinking creatively about date nights or family vacations or fun weekend activities. Your finger needs to be on the pulse of what the family needs.

You need to be reflective about behavioral issues with the children, how best to train them and provide the discipline that results in growth rather than exasperation. You need to initiate conversation about what kind of disobedience will get what kind of consequence.

You need to make informed decisions about educational choices for your children: public school, private school, home school. How will you navigate that, and why? You need to think through family finances, setting appropriate, God-honoring goals while devising a strategic plan to live within your means.

You need to be the one who addresses conflict first—not by blaming your wife for it but by breaking the silence and seeking peace. You must be the one to apologize and seek forgiveness first. You have to be the first one to say, "Something is amiss, and I hate it; I know I'm responsible for a portion of it. I don't want this to go on. Can we talk? Will you forgive me for . . . " whatever it might be.

One of the greatest temptations men face is either to avoid conflict or to turn everything into a conflict. We face this temptation either to be a cruel tyrant who has to turn everything into a fight until we get our way or to be a weak-willed wimp who runs from conflict, with no stomach for it.

But like a firefighter who runs toward the burning building while everyone else runs away, biblical men run toward conflict. That's not because a man loves conflict—not any more than a firefighter loves playing in burning buildings. It's because he is responsible to protect those under his charge from the damage an unaddressed conflict will inflict.

You need to brainstorm about how best to involve your family in the ministry of the local church, how you can come alongside fellow believers and meet their needs, and how you can be intentional in speaking the gospel to those the Lord has put in your life who do not yet know Him.

This is leadership. This is the delightful burden of being a man. It's not that a wife has nothing to say about these matters; no, she's given to you to help you in all of these things. Though the buck may stop with you, the good leader seeks the input of those he's leading. He understands their needs and even their preferences, and he will often adopt their ideas.

It's not that a woman can take no initiative. But the man bears the primary responsibility to lead. When facing a tough decision, he bears the burden of having the final say—the burden of knowing that God will hold him accountable if he fails to lead in paths of righteousness and wisdom.

So, eschewing the weakness of indecision and procrastination, the biblical man runs *toward* responsibility. His leadership is deferential but decisive. He solicits input from others to make a wise decision, and then he makes it. He's not impulsive, but neither is he paralyzed. He seeks God's help, studies the Scriptures, applies biblical wisdom, and moves forward.

Man Is a Lover

A second mark of biblical manhood is that he is a lover. That is, he is one who loves, affectionately and sacrificially. He exercises his leadership lovingly. In First Corinthians 16:13, Paul exhorted the church to "Be on the alert, stand firm in the faith, act like men, be strong."

As we will see in chapter 9, strength, courage, and fortitude are all attributes of biblical masculinity. But right after calling them to "act like men" and "be strong," his next words were, "Let all that you do be done in love" (16:14). There is an unmistakable connection between acting like a man and *loving*.

In Titus 2:2, Paul said that older men are to be sound in love. In First Timothy 1:5, Paul counseled Timothy that "the goal of our instruction is love from a pure heart and a good conscience and a sincere faith." Men of God who serve the church as pastors, who work hard at preaching and teaching, have love as the goal of all their labors.

Then, Paul applied this particularly to husbands when he said, "Husbands, love your wives and do not be embittered against them" (Col. 3:19). The parallel passage is that famous instruction on marriage in Ephesians 5:25–33, in which God says to husbands:

> Husbands, love your wives, just as Christ also loved the church, and gave Himself up for her, so that He might sanctify her, having cleansed her by the washing of water with the word, that He might present to Himself the church in all her glory, having no spot or wrinkle or any such thing; but that she would be holy and blameless. So husbands ought also to love their own wives as their own bodies. He who loves his own wife loves himself; for no one ever hated his own flesh, but nourishes and cherishes it, just

> as Christ also does the church, because we are members of His body. . . . Nevertheless, each individual among you also is to love his own wife even as himself, and the wife must see to it that she respects her husband.

The fertile soil of that passage has much for us to harvest. First, Paul pointed to Christ as the model for men who would be marked by love for their wives. The greatest Man who ever lived was love incarnate. Christ's love for His bride was the pattern for each husband's love for his bride.

Loving Sacrifice

Several features of Christ's love for the church prove instructive for husbands' love for their wives, but above all, Christ's love is characterized by sacrifice: "Husbands, love your wives, just as Christ also loved the church, and gave Himself up for her" (5:25).

The Lord Jesus Christ subordinated His own interests, convenience, and well-being to benefit His bride when He "did not regard equality with God a thing to be grasped, but emptied Himself [by] taking the form of a slave, and being made in the likeness of men . . . He humbled Himself by becoming obedient to the point of death, even death on a cross" (Phil. 2:6–8). The one who reclines at the table is greater than the one who serves, but the Lord of heaven and earth was among us "as the one who serves" (Luke 22:25–27). Our Savior showed us that leadership is loving. Headship is humble.

How did the Bridegroom of the church serve His bride? By ordering every aspect of His life to benefit His loved ones. And that wasn't just manifest in His death, though that was the greatest sacrifice ever made: Jesus bore the wrath of the God, whose smile He treasured and whose frown He never deserved to know. More than that, He lived every moment of His life in perfect, surrendered obedience to the Father, fulfilling the law on behalf of the lawbreakers He would justify (Matt. 3:15; Rom. 5:18–19; Gal. 4:4–5).

Jesus may have looked weak as the One who served everyone else, and who died a criminal's death. But it was nothing but pure, holy, manly strength that enabled Him to say no to the temptations of Satan, of the world that lay in Satan's power, and to say no to any preference of His own comfort or ease over and above the benefit of His church.

Dear brothers, consider how exquisitely you have been loved by Christ, your bridegroom—how noble, selfless, and sacrificial His love was and is to you. And then, beholding the glory of that sacrificial love, can you find your heart warmed by grace to love your wife like Christ loved you?

The occasion may never call for you to die in her place—though, if it did, it would mean gladly sacrificing your life for hers. But the kind of sacrificial love to which Paul calls you is *living* for her—not just in a singular romantic moment of heroism, as you knock her out of the way of a moving train or jump between her and a bullet. It's laying down your life in the day-by-day, moment-by-moment decisions of life together. It means sacrificing the fleshly comforts of idleness, ease, and recreation to benefit those you love and are responsible to lead.

It costs something to live a disciplined life of daily prayer and Bible study, so you can be a man worth following, a man who looks like Christ, who pleases Christ, and who has learned to lead like Christ.

That doesn't happen apart from communion with Christ. And that will mean saying "no" to extra sleep or extra leisure time. It may mean not catching up on that TV show or that hobby, because there's work to be done in the secret place, at the feet of Christ in His Word and in prayer. The costs include giving up those preferences and leisure activities to intentionally take the initiative in ways we noted earlier: planning family vacations, managing the budget, or taking care of other needs of the household. It means you sacrifice the freedom of being driven by your emotions or the spontaneity of the moment so that you live an ordered, disciplined, intentional life.

Home *to* Work

As an illustration, toward the end of the night, I often read or watch TV before bed and my wife will ask, "Do you feel like helping with the dishes?"

The honest answer is, "No, I feel like finishing this chapter or watching this episode." But that's because I'm a selfish person with the law of sin still waging war in my flesh. In that moment, "giving myself up for her" means getting off the couch and helping with the dishes.

Or I'll come home from a long day of ministry—perhaps wrestling with a biblical text and the best way to craft a sermon, or pleading in a counseling room with people stubbornly clinging to their sin, or praying for the needs of the flock. After a long drive in the purgatory of Los Angeles traffic, by the time I get home, I'm exhausted. I want to loaf around and be served!

But the kids want to play, and my wife wants help after caring for them all day. What does the man do? He lays down his preferences and his comfort, and he serves. Men don't go home *from* work; they go home *to* work. You go home, friend, to the good and noble work of giving yourself up in engaged, initiative-taking headship to serve your family. Why?

Because Jesus looked at His disciples and said, "I am among you as the one who serves."

It's been well-said that "the gospel makes men who hate selfishness and crave selflessness."[9]

Love Like the Second Adam

Mature, masculine, biblical love consists in sacrificially laying down your life to serve others. The Second Adam got this right, as we've seen. But the first Adam didn't.

In Genesis 3, one of the first results of Adam's abdication of his headship and fall into sin was to shift blame. God called Adam to account for what happened, and Adam said, "The woman whom You gave to be with me, she gave me from the tree, and I ate" (Gen. 3:12).

Such a disgusting display! Not long before, Adam had joyfully exclaimed, "Bone of my bones! Flesh of my flesh! This masterpiece shall be called Woman!" (Gen. 2:23). Now, he derisively referred to her as "the woman." I agree with the commentators who interpret this as Adam effectively saying, "It was her fault; kill her, not me."[10]

This was a cowardly abdication of Adam's headship, and men still struggle with that. The loving thing to do—the manly thing to do, the Second-Adam-like thing to do—would have been to give himself up for her: to stand between his wife and the Judge of all the earth and say, "Lord, I failed to lead my wife and keep her safe from temptation. Take me instead of her. It was my responsibility. I'll bear the guilt of her sin and mine."

A biblical man is loving. He doesn't make excuses for his sin and try to shift the blame onto someone else, least of all the good gift of a wife that the Lord has given him as a helper. Biblical men take responsibility; they lovingly sacrifice themselves for the benefit and protection of those they love—even being willing to shoulder the blame or the consequences for something they didn't do if it means protecting their loved ones from danger and delivering them unto blessing.

And why is that? Because that is the gospel, friends. That is what the Second Adam did. He succeeded in the way the first Adam failed—and in the way that each of Adam's sons has failed. He has given Himself up for sinners by dying for us on the cross, bearing the full weight of the curse due to us for our sins. He has risen again on the third day in victory, and He now

9 Strachan and Peacock, *The Grand Design*, 154.

10 Beeke and Smalley, *Reformed Systematic Theology*, 2:354.

calls every sinner come to Him and find forgiveness, righteousness, and rest for our souls.

You who have failed to be biblical men: come to the perfect Man, who pays the penalty for the failures of His people, who leads His own in sacrificial love, and who gives grace to make His own more and more like Himself. Trust in Him for pardon, and trust in Him for power to walk in obedience to this lofty calling of biblical manhood.

Study Questions:

1. The chapter claimed, "Women never flourish more than when men act like men." Do you agree? Why or why not?

2. What is your evaluation of our culture's concept of "toxic masculinity"? Is masculinity itself toxic? Are certain aspects of masculinity toxic? Support your answer with Scripture.

3. The past 150 years have included the greatest advances of the feminist movement. Has feminism succeeded in making humans flourish? Explain your answer.

4. In what ways does Scripture identify the man as the leader or head of the family?

5. Why did God call Adam to account when Eve sinned first?

6. Read "Leadership in Action" again. List three specific ways you need to grow in practical leadership of your family. For each, sketch a brief plan for how you'll improve over the next four weeks.

7. Why are indecision, procrastination, and fleeing conflict marks of abdicating leadership?

8. Given how Christ has loved you, what are three specific ways you can better love your wife and children sacrificially? See if you can connect specific gospel truths to specific principles for application.

9. If you were Adam, what would you have said when God called you to account for breaking His command? What implications does your answer have for the way you deal with sin and conflict in your marriage?

8

PROVIDER AND PROTECTOR

THE DELIGHTFUL DUTIES OF BIBLICAL MASCULINITY

THE LAST CHAPTER established that God made man to be a leader, one who takes responsibility and gives direction. We also found that such leadership is thoroughly loving, marked by the man's willing sacrifice to benefit those he leads.

MAN IS A PROVIDER

Loving leadership is also marked by providing for those you lead. We see that perhaps most clearly in Ephesians 5, where Paul made Christ's love for the church the pattern for the husband's love for his wife.

In addition to Ephesians 5:25, which sets forth the general principle, verses 28 and 29 read, "So husbands ought also to love their own wives as their own bodies. He who loves his own wife loves himself; for no one ever hated his own flesh, but nourishes and cherishes it, just as Christ also does the church."

Christ nourishes and cherishes the church because she is "his own flesh"—the body of Christ, His bride. In the same way, a man's loving headship over his wife must be marked by nourishing and cherishing her. Both of these words give insight into what it means for a man to be a provider.

The term "nourish" translates the Greek word *ektrephō,* used only in Ephesians 5:29 and 6:4 in the New Testament. The latter occurrence speaks of fathers bringing their children up in the discipline and instruction of the Lord. The word appears often in the Greek translation of the Old Testament, always in the context of either raising children (1 Kings 11:20; 2 Kings 10:6; Isa. 23:4; Hos. 9:12) or providing for the needs of others (Gen. 47:17; 2 Sam. 12:3).

A helpful illustration comes in Genesis 45, when Joseph consoled his brothers who had sold him into slavery in Egypt. He didn't hold this against them but recognized God's sovereign purpose to preserve life through the famine, and he wanted them to settle in Goshen. He said, "There I will also provide for you, for there are still five years of famine to come, lest you and your household and all that you have be impoverished" (v. 11). Joseph said there was a famine coming, but he would nourish his family. He would arrange for their needs to be met and they wouldn't starve.

The apostle Paul says this is the responsibility of the husband toward the wife. The man must see to it that the physical needs of his wife and family are met—that there is food on the table and clothes on their backs.

He must also "cherish" her. The term *thalpō* literally means "to make warm," but in the sense of "to care for." Similar to the previous, it's used only one other place in the New Testament, when a person "tenderly cares for" his own child (1 Thess. 2:7). For a father to care for his children and "make them warm," means he ensures they are clothed and sheltered, instead of being destitute and "left out in the cold."

A husband cherishes his wife, then, when he tenderly cares for her physical needs, similar to the way a loving mother does whatever is necessary to care for her child. The emphasis isn't on the husband parenting the wife, of course, but on totally giving of himself to provide for her needs.

Providing for Physical Needs

A man is to provide for both the physical and spiritual needs. As we've seen, physical provision is the most natural sense of "nourish" and "cherish" in Ephesians 5. That is confirmed by the teaching of the opening chapters of Genesis, which are so foundational in the study of human identity. After describing the creation of man from the dust, and then some of the beautiful features of the lush garden of Eden, Genesis 2:15 says, "Then Yahweh God took the man and put him into the garden of Eden to cultivate it and keep it"—literally, to work it, and to watch over it.

First of all, note that God put man into the garden to work. From the beginning of man's existence, before his fall into sin, he was created to be a worker. Work is not a product of the curse. Man did not become a worker after the fall. His work got more difficult, but work is not the product of sin. Work is a man's natural element. It is his original environment. And don't forget: That original environment was paradise! That seems strange to us, since we live in a culture that idolizes idleness, leisure, recreation, and retirement. But work was a part of the original paradise.

Man is a worker. We were created to be employed: to rule and subdue the earth according to God's mandate; to partner with the God who completed

His work of creation on the sixth day and rested from work on the seventh (Gen. 2:2); to partner with the God of whom Jesus said, "My Father is working until now, and I Myself am working" (John 5:17). We are to work along with Him in such a way that through our labors, the rest of the earth reflects the order, beauty, and glory of the garden of Eden (Gen. 1:26–28).

Men, one of our chief pitfalls in this life is the temptation to laziness, procrastination, indolence, and an undisciplined life. Sin inclines us to view work as a necessary evil, rather than a blessing from heaven. The Bible tells us that when we get lazy and run from our responsibility to work, we act against something native to our God-given constitution as men.

Biblical men are not lazy; they are hard workers. You need to fight the temptation to slothfulness by considering that work is part of your identity, part of who God created you to be. The Lord your God has created you to work hard, precisely so that you can earn enough money to provide for the needs of those whom God entrusts to you to nourish and cherish—especially your wife.

Clues from the Curse

We see this even in the way the curse comes upon the man and the woman. In response to their sin, God cursed the man and the woman in different ways, according to their roles and spheres of responsibility. He cursed the woman with respect to her domestic relationships—first with respect to childbearing and then, in her relationship to her husband: "To the woman He said, / 'I will greatly multiply / Your pain in childbirth, / in pain you will bring forth children'" (3:16).

Then God said, "Your desire will be for your husband, and he will rule over you." Her desire will be for her husband in the same way that sin's desire was for Cain (4:7)—namely, to rule over him. The woman was not cursed with the role of submission; that predated the fall. She was cursed with discontentment in her role of submission, to the degree that she would want to occupy her husband's role and rule over him, in a way that would breed conflict.

Then, God cursed the man with respect to his vocation as a worker of the ground: "Cursed is the ground because of you; in toil you will eat of it all the days of your life. Both thorns and thistles it shall grow for you; And you will eat the plants of the field; by the sweat of your face you will eat bread, till you return to the ground" (3:17–19). While God didn't curse Adam with work, He cursed him within his natural domain as a worker, within the role He had already created him to occupy. What would have been a delight and brought blessing now is difficult, painful, and toilsome.

God cursed the woman with respect to her natural, pre-fall domain, which was to be a help to her husband and to bear and rear children. She was to be a worker at home (Titus 2:5). And He cursed the man with respect to his natural, pre-fall domain, which was to engage in breadwinning labor to provide for his wife and family. The primary burden for putting food on the table and a roof over the heads of the family falls to the husband.

That does not mean women cannot work, or even that there aren't seasons when a wife would work outside the home.[1] But it does mean a husband should never willingly put his wife in a position to feel the pressure of having to earn money so the family can survive. She has other responsibilities she must tend to for the family's survival; she should not also feel the burden of this one.

The man is the one who lays down his life in diligent, sacrificial labor to provide for his family's needs. John Piper put it this way:

> When there is no bread on the table it is the man who should feel the main pressure to do something to get it there. . . . A man will feel his [manhood] compromised if he, through sloth or folly or lack of discipline, becomes dependent over the long haul (not just during graduate school!) on his wife's income.[2]

Providing When Single

But what if you're not married? How can men discharge their duty of physical provision without a wife?

You can still work hard at whatever the Lord has given you to do (Eccles. 9:10). You can develop a strong work ethic and habits that will put you in a position to secure a job that will provide for a family one day. You can study diligently as you pursue a vocation that will allow you to be depended on as the one who bears primary responsibility for physical provision.

Your attitude cannot be, "Well, I don't have a wife or kids to provide for, so I can work part-time and take it easy." If that's your attitude toward work, you may never have a wife and kids to support. But further, you weren't made to take it easy! You were made to work hard for six days and rest on one. You can apply this teaching even as a single man by the way you prepare to be a provider.

More than that, men can apply this principle even in contexts with women who are not their wives. That man is a provider by nature means it's

1 Piper, *This Momentary Marriage*, 87.

2 Piper, *What's the Difference?*, 39.

right for a man to pay for dinner on a date. Or, if you are out with a group of friends and one forgets her wallet, it's fitting for a guy to pay for her meal.

It's right for men to make themselves useful enough to help other friends with fixing things around the house—especially those tasks that a husband or a father would usually take care of. For example, an older single lady came to our church leadership for help. She needed someone to advocate for her in the midst of a dispute, the way a husband might do if he were in the picture.

One of the young men in the church went with her and helped her. That was a way of providing for her physical needs—not because she was part of the same household, but because she was part of the household of faith. This is just one example of how a single man can be a provider.

Providing for Spiritual Needs

But Scripture also calls men to provide for spiritual needs. In the same way, brothers, that you are responsible to put food on the table so that the family is well-nourished, you are also responsible to put spiritual food on the table, so that the family is sustained by the blessings of the Word of God and the means of grace.

Ephesians 5 teaches that, as well. Husbands are called to love their wives after the pattern of Christ's love for the church—who "gave Himself up for her, so that He might sanctify her, having cleansed her by the washing of water with the word, that He might present to Himself the church in all her glory, having no spot or wrinkle or any such thing; but that she would be holy and blameless" (5:25–27). Christ's purpose in giving Himself up in sacrificial love for His bride was to purify and sanctify her. His aim was her moral excellence.

Now, husbands cannot sanctify their wives in the same way Christ does the church. But they are to be a sanctifying influence upon their wives. Men, you are to order your life in the service of your wife's spiritual growth. You must be strategic in plotting ways to see your wife grow in appropriating the means of grace, to see her pursue deeper communion with Christ, to put off patterns and habits of sin, and to put on patterns and habits of righteousness. You are to provide for her spiritually.

We also see this in the early chapters of Genesis. Genesis 2:15–17 described God giving Adam the command not to eat from the tree, and then creating the woman in the next paragraph (2:18). God entrusted Adam with the responsibility to be Eve's teacher of the word of God.[3] He was to

3 Beeke and Smalley, *Reformed Systematic Theology*, 2:212.

instruct her concerning the command the Lord had given him, and to see that she applied it in the way God intended.

Adam failed miserably at that, of course! But the original design was for the man to instruct his wife in the ways of Yahweh. The apostle Paul reaffirmed this when he instructed women to remain silent in church: "If they desire to learn anything, let them ask their own husbands at home" (1 Cor. 14:35). Husbands are to be competent enough in the Scriptures to answer their wives' questions about spiritual matters.

And it's not only their wives. In Ephesians 6:1, Paul commanded children to obey their parents, and he used that generic term *goneús* to speak of both mother and father. But then, in verse 4, he specifically charged fathers *(hoi patéres)* to bring up their children in the discipline and instruction of the Lord. Now, of course mothers are to teach their children a host of things—including about the Lord and His Word. But this text teaches us that the fathers have a special responsibility to provide for the spiritual growth and maturity of their children.

Practical Provision

This means a biblical man is a man of God. Brothers, you need to be a man who knows, studies, loves, and practices the Word of God, so that you might know your God and make Him known to those in your spiritual charge.

You are to be a man of prayer—of private prayer; a man like Jacob, who wrestles with the Lord on your knees, who refuses to let go of Him until you are blessed with the light of the Lord's countenance upon you (Gen. 32:36; Num. 6:24–26), so that you may go forth from the secret place transformed by that glory (2 Cor. 3:18), with the light of that glory reflecting off of you, to be a sanctifying influence on those you're entrusted to lead. You are to be a man who wages war against his own flesh and puts off sin and puts on righteousness (Rom. 8:12–13).

You are to be an exemplary man, as Paul exhorted young men, "In all things show yourself to be an example of good deeds" (Titus 2:7). You are to set the spiritual pace for your family and others—a pattern that can be reliably followed. You can say with Paul, "Be imitators of me, just as I also am of Christ" (1 Cor. 11:1). You're to be a man who not only practices what you preach, but a man who practices *before* you preach—because you recognize that the power of example often far outweighs the power of precept.

Being a spiritual provider means leading in family worship. You are to take initiative in gathering the family for Bible reading, prayer, and singing to the Lord. Structure your home around studying the Word of God and praying together. You are to consistently pray for the sanctification of your wife and children, offering specific petitions for their growth in specific areas. That means you have your finger on the pulse of their spiritual needs, and you take those needs to the throne of grace and plead with Christ to reign in their lives.

You are to lead your family to regular, vital participation in the local church. That means you will make it unthinkable for someone in your house to wake up on Sunday morning and ask, "Are we going to church today?" They should know your response will be, "Of course we are! It's the Lord's Day! We get to gather with the people of God! We hear the skilled preaching of the Word! We get to have fellowship with our brothers and sisters!"

Being a spiritual provider means making the spiritual atmosphere of your home one of discipleship. In Deuteronomy 6:7, Moses charged the people of God to teach His Word diligently to their children—to talk of His words when you sit in your house and when you walk by the way and when you lie down and when you rise up. This means driving the topics of conversation back to spiritual things, discussing moral and ethical issues, teaching your children how to assess the events of the day through a biblical worldview.

It also means taking the initiative in discipline. In Hebrews 12, as the author urges us to receive the Lord's discipline as from a loving father, he assumes that fathers lead in administering discipline to the children: "For what son is there whom his father does not discipline?" (12:7). "We had earthly fathers to discipline us" (12:9).

That doesn't mean mothers don't administer discipline, but fathers take the initiative to bring correction and instruction to the children when necessary. A husband should never sit passively by while his wife deals with an openly misbehaving child because he is too lazy to deal with the child.

Man Is a Protector

A fourth mark of biblical manhood is that man is a protector. Genesis 2:15 tells us God put Adam in the garden "to cultivate it and keep it."

The word translated "keep" (Hebrew, *shāmar*) carries the connotation not only of maintaining the garden but watching over it. The same word is used to speak of the flaming sword that Yahweh stationed at the entrance of the garden of Eden "to guard the way to the tree of life" (Gen. 3:24). It's used several times in the book of Job to speak of God "watching over" him (29:2; 13:27; 33:11). So, Adam was to guard the garden. He was to watch over it. Being a protector was native to his existence from the very beginning.

We also see this principle in Ephesians 5. When we read that "Christ . . . loved the church and gave Himself up for her," we need to remember what that "giving up" entailed. It meant the innocent Lord Jesus stepped in between His guilty bride and omnipotent Justice.

God's wrath burned hot against sinners and threatened to break over our heads in the infinite horrors of eternal hell. We were in the gravest danger imaginable. And what did Christ, our Bridegroom, do? He stood in front of us and bore our condemnation in our place. "He was pierced through for our transgressions. He was crushed for our iniquities" (Isa. 53:4). "Christ redeemed us from the curse of the Law, having become a curse for us" (Gal. 3:13).

He died for us so that we would be "saved from the wrath of God through Him" (Rom. 5:9). There has been no greater demonstration of protection in the history of the world than the way Christ protected His bride from the wrath of God that she so richly deserved. And so, when Paul called husbands to love our wives like Christ loved the church, he called us, at the very least, to protect them at all costs.[4]

Protecting against Physical Danger

And just as a biblical man provides both physically and spiritually, he also protects both physically and spiritually. Men are to provide physical protection for women and children—and especially for their own families. If thee is a physical threat of any kind, "mature masculinity senses a natural, God-given responsibility to step forward and put himself between" that threat and the one he's protecting.[5]

This has so many applications that it's hard to know how to illustrate it well, but I've always appreciated this one. If you and your wife are in bed at night and it sounds like someone may be breaking into the house, you don't turn to your wife and say, "Honey, we're equal image-bearers of God. In Christ there is neither male nor female. I wouldn't demean your self-worth by insisting that I go check on that noise. I went last time, and this is an egalitarian marriage, so let me know how it goes." It doesn't matter if you're 5'3" and 120 pounds, and your wife holds a black belt in jiujitsu; it's hardwired into your soul that, as the man, you go and protect your wife.[6]

4 Piper, *This Momentary Marriage*, 86.

5 Piper, *What's the Difference?*, 41.

6 Piper, *This Momentary Marriage*, 91.

But it doesn't have to just be in the marriage relationship. If another man is physically threatening a woman, whether she's related to you or not, the manly thing to do is to divert the threat from her to yourself. That can mean walking a classmate or a co-worker to her car when it's dark outside. It means standing on the street side of the sidewalk. And it has nothing to do with capacity or competency. John Piper put that helpfully when he said, "Women and children are put into the lifeboats first, not because the men are necessarily better swimmers, but because of a deep sense of honorable fitness. It belongs to masculinity to accept danger to protect women."[7]

In July 2020, a six-year-old boy from Wyoming named Bridger Walker saw a German Shepherd charging at his four-year-old sister, and he instinctively jumped between her and the dog. The German Shepherd bit him numerous times in the face and on the head.

The boy survived, but he received 90 stitches in his face—he'll always have the scars. When his family asked why he put himself in harm's way to protect his sister, he said, "If someone had to die, I thought it should be me."[8] Though he was only six years old, that boy behaved more like a man than many of the adult males heralded as heroes and role models today.

"It belongs to masculinity to accept danger to protect women." It doesn't matter how strong you are or what size you are. It matters that God has made men to be protectors. And just like that was true for our Savior, we should reason that, if someone has to die, it should be us men, and not our wives, sisters, mothers, or daughters.

Protecting against Spiritual Danger

Not only are men to provide physical protection, they are also to provide spiritual protection. In Paul's classic exhortation to "act like men" and "be strong" (1 Cor. 16:13), the first command in that series is, "Be on the alert."

Men are commanded to be spiritually watchful. You are to have an alertness, a sobriety, a readiness, so you can spy out the spiritual dangers that threaten those you're charged to lead, issue warnings, and perhaps even intervene, so that no spiritual harm comes to your loved ones.

---

7 Piper, *What's the Difference?*, 42.

8 Joelle Goldstein, "Hero Boy Who Saved Sister in Dog Attack Feels Face Scar Is 'Something to Be Proud Of,' Says Dad," https://people.com/human-interest/wyoming-boy-bridger-walker-who-saved-sister-in-dog-attack-feels-proud-of-scar-says-dad (accessed December 2023).

The spiritual dangers that threaten the Christian family are ever present. We find them in the wicked, demonic thinking of the secular culture that assaults minds through movies, TV, Internet, and the news. But we also find them in false teaching of professing Christian teachers that threaten to corrupt our understanding of sound doctrine.

This means men must "hold fast the faithful word which is in accordance with the teaching, so that [you] will be able both to exhort in sound doctrine and to refute those who contradict" (Titus 1:9).

Men, you must know theology. You must know what the Bible teaches about God, Christ, the Holy Spirit, and the Scriptures; about mankind, sin, and salvation; about the church, spiritual gifts, men's and women's roles; and about the last things. Why? So you can teach your family the truth and protect your family from error—which, if embraced, shipwrecks faith and destroys the soul. Paul instructed "older men" to be "sound in faith" (Titus 2:2), which is to be sound in *the* faith—in that body of doctrine that was delivered to the saints (Jude 1:3). Then he told the "young men" that they must have "purity in doctrine" (Titus 2:7).

Brothers, you are to be the resident theologian in your home, so that when Satan, who prowls about like a roaring lion seeking whom he may devour, takes a run at your family—whether through temptation to corrupt doctrine or corrupt practice—you can resist him and protect them.

That protection will often come in the form of bringing words of correction. If your wife or your children are being taken in by some false teaching or are tempted to some pattern of unrighteous behavior, you need to correct them graciously and patiently. You must exercise the loving wisdom that Paul spoke about in Galatians 6:1: "If anyone is caught in any trespass, you who are spiritual, restore such a one in a spirit of gentleness; each one looking to yourself, so that you too will not be tempted." In humility, mindful of your own faults, you go to seek the benefit of your wife or your children, knowing that if they persist in courses dishonoring to God, they will forfeit His blessing.

Unchecked, unrepentant sin brings spiritual misery. You don't want that for them. Even if it's uncomfortable, time-consuming, and presents the potential for conflict, you protect your family by offering wise and loving correction.

Being a spiritual protector also means laboring in prayer for your wife and children—praying that the Lord will not lead them into temptation but deliver them from evil (Matt. 6:13); praying that He would lift up the light of His countenance upon them and give them peace (Num. 6:24–26); praying that He would satisfy them in the morning with His lovingkindness (Ps. 90:14), that they would live in single-minded devotion to Him (Ps. 27:4).

It also requires you to set standards for what TV shows, movies, and music will be allowed in the home. It will mean setting standards for what clothing will and will not be worn, explaining principles of modesty, ensuring that everything appropriate is done so your wife and your daughters are protected from becoming the objects of the lustful glances of unprincipled men, and "telling them when the way they dress means what they don't think [or don't realize] it means."[9]

Being a spiritual protector means taking initiative to seek reconciliation amid conflict. If you know a relational breakdown has occurred, you can't let that strife fester, or it will turn into bitterness. Men take the lead to resolve conflict; they race to say, "I'm sorry. Will you please forgive me?" They don't sit back with their arms folded, pouting childishly about how "She needs to apologize because it was her fault!" They cultivate an entreatable, Christlike spirit that is eager to grant forgiveness as soon as it's asked, so the sun doesn't go down on anyone's anger, and the devil is given no opportunity (Eph. 4:26–27).

A Grace-Fueled Battle

The biblical man is a leader, a lover, a provider, and a protector. And the provision and protection he furnishes to his wife and family is both physical and spiritual. This is what we must practice, men. This is the standard God's Word sets out for us to fulfill our calling as men made in the image of God. This is how God has designed us.

Though we fall woefully short of that design because of the corruption of sin, remember, brothers, in Christ we have redemption from those very transgressions, so that their penalty is paid and their power is broken. We look forward to the day when even the presence of such sins are eradicated—from ourselves and from the entire creation—so Christ will finally have what He is worthy of from us. But until then, we walk in the strength of blood-bought forgiveness, of imputed righteousness, to engage in the Spirit-empowered, grace-filled fight for holiness.

We have been raised with Christ to walk in newness of life. Where we see our deficiencies, our failures, and our sins unmortified, we can go before the Lord in prayer and battle with our flesh, nailing that remaining sin to

9 Piper, *This Momentary Marriage*, 91.

the cross, and putting it away from ourselves, unto the honor of our King. Then we can be the men that He has re-created us to be. May God grant that we would be men.

Study Questions:

1. How do the terms "nourish" and "cherish" speak of a man's duty to provide for his wife and family?
2. What is your attitude toward work? According to the chapter, what *should* be your attitude toward work? What needs to happen to make those answers the same?
3. How does God's curse identify the primary "domains" of men and women, respectively?
4. In what scenarios do you believe it is allowable for a wife to work outside the home? In what scenarios do you believe it is not acceptable for a wife to work outside the home?
5. What are some ways, other than those mentioned in the chapter, that a single man can fulfill his calling to be a provider?
6. In view of your duty to provide spiritually, assess your current state of spiritual discipline. What must change for you to read Scripture and pray more regularly? What practical steps will you take to achieve change?
7. What are some appropriate ways a husband offers physical protection to his wife? What are some appropriate ways a single man offers physical protection to women?
8. On a scale of 1 to 10, rate your performance as the spiritual protector of your home. Also ask your wife to rate you. Discuss the similarity or divergence of your answers, and brainstorm together about how to improve.
9. Talk with your wife about the spiritual influence movies, music, and other entertainment have on your home. Does anything need to change?
10. When conflict has resulted in lack of communication, why should you as the man pursue your wife before she pursues you?

9

Strong, Sensible, and Sound

The Character of Biblical Headship

THE LAST TWO CHAPTERS established that a biblical man is a leader, a lover, a provider, and a protector. This chapter will round out the discussion with several other marks of biblical manhood.

A Man is Strong

A fifth mark of biblical manhood is that he is strong. First Corinthians 16:13 provides ample support for this point. In a series of concluding exhortations to a Corinthian church riddled with problems and persecutions, Paul wrote, "Be on the alert, stand firm in the faith, act like men, be strong."

What does the Bible say it means to "act like men"? At the very least, it means to be strong. But "strong" in what sense?

Physical Strength

Paul drew upon familiar phraseology that was common in the Greek translation of the Old Testament, from which Paul often quoted. The verb translated "act like men" is *andrizomai.* It's the word for "man" *(andros)* turned from a noun into a verb. It literally means, "Be men," or, we might say more colloquially, "Man up." "Act like men" is a good translation. The word translated "be strong" is *krataióomai*; literally, "be strengthened" or "become strong."

These two words appear together in the Septuagint several times. When the Philistines had just routed Israel in battle, they heard the shouts of God's people rejoicing that the ark of the covenant had been returned to Israel, and they feared the presence of the true God. So to stir themselves up to battle with courage, they used these same words Paul used: "Take courage and be men, O Philistines, or you will become slaves to the Hebrews, as they have been slaves to you; therefore, be men and fight" (1 Sam. 4:9).

This is a battle cry, a call to war. In Second Samuel 10, the armies of Israel were flanked by the Ammonites on the one side and the Arameans on the other. Joab, the commander, stirred them up with this same battle cry: "Be strong [*andrizomai*], and let us show ourselves courageous [*krataióomai*] for the sake of our people and for the cities of our God" (2 Sam. 10:12).

The familiar refrain throughout the book of Joshua—"Be strong and courageous" (Josh. 1:6, 7, 9, 18; 10:25)—is close to the phrase in First Corinthians 16:13. It uses the term *andrizomai* for "be courageous," but then uses a synonym of *krataióomai* for "be strong": *ischúō*. It's a different word, but it carries essentially the same meaning. And in fact, the phrase *andros ischuros*—the noun and adjective forms of the verbs *andrizomai* and *ischúō*—is often translated "valiant warrior" in the Old Testament (e.g., Dan. 3:20). So Paul drew a familiar phrase from God's Word to call the Corinthian church to display manly courage that one would have to display as he roused himself for hand-to-hand combat to the death.

We can conclude that the strength Paul called us to when he told us to "act like men" is marked both by physical strength and courage. If these terms are used to describe valiant warriors, it's no stretch to say that biblical men are to be physically strong.

God designed men to be the ones employed in physical labor, and, if necessary, even physical altercation, under righteous circumstances. On average, men have denser bones, larger hearts, and greater muscle mass than women.[1] They can usually run faster, lift heavier weights, and outperform women in combat situations.[2]

God has designed us, then, as men, to steward those natural gifts of creation and to keep our bodies healthy and strong, so we might be both the provider and the protector that God calls us to be—strong enough to work hard to provide for our families and strong enough to protect them, should they meet physical danger.

It's not that every "real man" has to lift weights, climb mountains, and be a mixed-martial artist. There are plenty of overgrown boys with chiseled bodies. But part of the Bible's prescription for men to be strong is to steward the natural strength God has given us as men by keeping ourselves

1 Luke Griffo, *The Beauty of the Binary: Male and Female He Created Them* (Cape Coral, FL: Founders Press, 2022), 28.

2 Strachan and Peacock, *The Grand Design*, 30.

physically fit. That means having the discipline to control our appetites; the discipline to eat well and exercise, and to mortify patterns of indulgence and laziness. It means we keep ourselves strong to provide for and protect those God has entrusted us to lead.

One other word about that. Though biblical men should be physically strong, we should never be bullies. The sinful, secular world has corrupted the good gift of strength. Physical strength in an unregenerate man is often perverted into an obnoxious, self-aggrandizing boastfulness—a cocky, condescending arrogance that takes advantage of weak people. That is not manly. It's the opposite of manly. It is the loud weakness of little boys who have grown physically but who have not grown in character. Masculine strength is to be harnessed, exercised with self-control and in proportion, in order to serve others for *their* benefit, not to subjugate others for *our* benefit. The truest, noblest strength is meekness, best defined as strength under control.

And the greatest example of that, of course, is Jesus. As to His strength, He was Almighty God incarnate. He healed diseases with a touch (Luke 5:12–13). He stilled the seas with a word (Matt. 8:26). He subdued demons by His own command (Mark 1:25–26). He could call down legions of angels to destroy His earthly enemies—but He didn't (Matt. 26:53–54). That strength was under His sovereign control. One writer captures it elegantly:

> This all-powerful God-man dealt gently with His disciples, who were but dust. He bore patiently with the faithless and twisted generation into which He was born. He graciously restored His followers who had abandoned Him, not the least of whom were the likes of Peter and Thomas. He allowed Himself to be arrested by thugs, farcically tried, mocked, and abused by those "strong men" around Him, and hung on a cross before breathing His last rather than calling upon the legions of angels at His disposal.[3]

The greatest Man who ever lived, the Man who was the epitome of strength, was strong enough to keep His strength under control. He did not use His power as an abusive chauvinist but as a gentle and humble servant, one who would rather bear pain than inflict it on others.

Moral Strength

That leads us to observe that the strength we're called to is not just physical strength. The battle for which Paul calls the church to "act like men" and

3 Griffo, *The Beauty of the Binary*, 55–56.

"be strong" isn't a physical battle like it had been for Israel. It's a spiritual battle, and it calls for moral strength—the kind of courage and fortitude that (as the verse also says) stands firm in the face of danger, that refuses to fold at the threats of persecution, and that will not compromise faithfulness because of what it costs.

A great illustration of moral strength comes in First Kings 2. "As David's time to die drew near, he charged Solomon his son, saying, 'I am going the way of all the earth. Be strong, therefore, and show yourself a man'" (2:1–2). Familiar language to us by now. But what did that manly strength entail, in David's mind? He continued,

> Keep the charge of Yahweh your God, to walk in His ways, to keep His statutes, His commandments, His ordinances, and His testimonies, according to what is written in the law of Moses, that you may succeed in all that you do and wherever you turn, so that Yahweh may carry out His promise which He spoke concerning me. (2:3–4)

The truest biblical strength is the strength to obey—to walk in accordance with God's commands. It involves the courage to renounce the world, the fortitude to resist the devil, and the resolve to mortify the flesh. A man is never weaker than when he rejects the commandment of God and yields to the power of sin. The strongest man in the room is the godliest man in the room.

I've mentioned one application of such moral strength in the previous chapters: Strong men don't run from conflict. They don't relish conflict; they don't seek out or instigate conflict. But they don't flee from it, either. In fact, they run to it. A police officer runs toward the sound of gunfire while everyone else runs away. He does that not because he loves getting shot at, but because he knows it falls to him to neutralize the threat. While everyone else may flee from unresolved conflict, the biblical man is strong enough to run to the conflict, in order to resolve it biblically.

A second application is that strong men receive correction well. They're strong enough not to let their egos get in the way of their sanctification. They're not discouraged or debilitated by criticism or correction, even if it's not offered well.

Strong men welcome correction, because their greatest desire is to please the Lord in all things, and they know they don't always see their own failures. They rejoice when the Lord uses another brother or sister to expose sin in their lives, because now they can work to be rid of that.

Strong men understand Proverbs 12:1: "Whoever loves discipline loves knowledge, but he who hates reproof is stupid." They believe Proverbs 15:32: "He who neglects discipline despises himself, but he who listens to reproof acquires understanding."

So far from being offended by criticism—so that he either wallows in self-pity or lashes out in anger—the strong man *invites* correction. He says with David, "Let the righteous smite me in kindness and reprove me; it is oil upon the head; do not let my head refuse it" (Ps. 141:5). The reproof of the righteous is like anointing oil that refreshes the head. That's the way a strong man talks.

A Man Is Sensible

In the sixth place, a biblical man is not only strong, but he is also sensible. And we see this emphasized in Titus 2. Paul's letter to Titus gave the apostle's directions to the young pastor to "set in order what remains" (1:5) in the establishment of the church on the island of Crete.

After setting out the qualifications of an elder (1:6–11), Paul exhorted Titus to "speak the things which are fitting for sound doctrine" (2:1). Then came instructions for the various demographics of the church: older men (2:2), older women (2:3), young women (2:4–5), young men (2:6–8), and slaves (2:9–10). And in the exhortations to older men and young men, Paul said they were to be sensible: "Older men are to be temperate, dignified, sensible" (2:2); "Likewise urge the young men to be sensible" (2:6).

This term, *sōphronéō*, means "to be of sound mind" (2 Cor 5:13),[4] or "to think so as to have sound judgment" (Rom. 12:3). It speaks of a strength of mind that is able to exercise discretion and discernment.

This is to say that a man is a thinking person. He's reasonable. He has a sense of himself and a sense of what's going on around him. He's dialed in, not aloof. He's not driven along by the wind and the waves of his circumstances, but his discretion allows him to discern what's going on around him and to make principled decisions that may go against the grain.

How contrary that is to the image of manhood portrayed in the culture. The media often portray men as checked out, helpless and hapless, grunts who go to work to earn a living, who then come home only to be overwhelmed by the demands of their families. Ray Romano's character in *Everybody Loves Raymond* is a good example of that. He's funny and goofy, but all he really

4 George W. Knight, III, *The Pastoral Epistles*, New International Greek Testament Commentary (Grand Rapids: Eerdmans, 1992), 310.

cares about is sports, food, time with the guys, and a merely physical relationship with his wife.

Years ago, Bill Cosby put his finger on this popular view of men when he said in one of his stand-up routines, "Fathers always say the same thing: 'Where's your mother?'" And he joked about how the father didn't know where anything was in the house, and how if you asked him to do something, he intentionally messed it up so everyone would realize he was useless and wouldn't bother him for anything else.

That is the opposite of what it means to be sensible. The sensible man is a thinking man, who has a sense of himself and what's going on around him, so that he is able to lead well.

Another connotation of *sōphronéō* is to be self-controlled. The term speaks of self-mastery. This is someone who has learned how to control his instincts and his passions.

A biblical man is not driven by his emotions. He's not impetuous or reckless, running headlong in one direction one day and then reversing course and going 90 miles-an-hour in the other direction the next day. He doesn't fly by the seat of his pants. He's a planner. He sets biblical goals, and then he takes the time to plot out how to achieve those goals in a way that maximizes efficiency and brings the most glory to God. Then, he sticks to that plan (or makes prudent adjustments), and therefore, brings stability into his own life and the lives of those he leads. Nothing is worse than trying to follow someone who's moving in fifteen different directions, depending on the day. But a sensible man has a steadying influence on those he leads.

That self-control also extends to controlling anger. A biblical man doesn't fly off the handle. He is not easily provoked. He heeds James's admonition that "everyone must be quick to hear, slow to speak, and slow to anger," knowing that "the anger of man does not achieve the righteousness of God" (James 1:19–20). He lives out the truth of Proverbs 16:32: "He who is slow to anger is better than the mighty, and he who rules his spirit, than he who captures a city."

The sensible man rules his spirit; he is not ruled *by* his spirit. He mortifies rage, anger, and brawling (Eph. 4:31). He puts to death those outbursts of anger that Paul includes in the list of the deeds of the flesh (Gal. 5:20).

The biblical man controls his temper. You don't hear him say things like, "Well, she just made me so angry that I . . . " No, it's juvenile weakness that surrenders control of one's temper to others.

A man is not driven into sin by anger; he's sensible, of sound mind. He rules his spirit, and he acts in accordance with sound judgment.

And that same self-control also extends to a man's purity, to controlling lusts. I'm not sure there is a greater ruiner of men than lust. Jesus said, "The eye is the lamp of the body; so then if your eye is clear, your whole body will be full of light. But if your eye is bad, your whole body will be full of darkness. If then the light that is in you is darkness, how great is the darkness!" (Matt. 6:23–24).

If you yield yourself to the lust of the eyes, giving unrestrained free rein to indulging your lusts, your mind and conscience become defiled (Titus 1:15). You become a lecher. You become one who cannot see women as sisters to be served but only objects to be used.

The world tells you it's manly to ogle women, to give full vent to your lusts. And women without respect for themselves are flattered by such things; they lust after being lusted after, so they make it easy for men to disgrace themselves.

But the world's way is hell's way, and it leads only to death (Prov. 2:18). The lustful man follows the adulteress "until an arrow pierces through his liver; as a bird hastens to the snare, so he does not know that it will cost him his life" (Prov. 7:23).

But the sensible man doesn't hasten to a snare. He flees youthful lusts, and pursues righteousness, faith, love, and peace (2 Tim. 2:22), because he knows this is God's will.

> For this is the will of God, your sanctification; that is, that you abstain from sexual immorality; that each of you know how to possess his own vessel [i.e., his own body] in sanctification and honor, not in lustful passion, like the Gentiles who do not know God; and that no man transgress and defraud his brother in the matter. … For God has not called us for the purpose of impurity, but in sanctification. (1 Thess. 4:3–7)

The world lies to us and says real men sleep with lots of women, are admired by many women, and have the affection of many women. Paul says real men are sensible. They have developed self-mastery and self-control over their passions; they possess their bodies in sanctification and honor, and they don't defraud one another by taking advantage of their sisters. They think, so as to have sound judgment.

So, brothers, be reasonable. If the sexually immoral will not inherit the kingdom of God (1 Cor. 6:9–10), and if the pure in heart shall see God (Matt. 5:8), then the only sensible thing to do is to discipline yourself for the purpose of godliness (1 Tim. 4:7).

A MAN IS DIGNIFIED

A seventh mark of biblical manhood is that a biblical man is dignified. Once again, Paul commanded Titus to exhort both older men and younger men to cultivate this grace. Titus 2:2: "Older men are to be temperate, dignified." And Titus 2:7: "In all things show yourself to be an example of good deeds, with purity in doctrine, dignified . . . "

The word is *semnos*, or sometimes *semnotēs*, used only a handful of times in the New Testament, and all but one of these usages are in the pastoral epistles. In First Timothy 2:2, Paul instructed us to pray for our leaders, "so that we may lead a tranquil and quiet life in all godliness and dignity." In the list of elder qualifications, he said an elder must keep "his children under control with all dignity" (1 Tim. 3:4). He made it a qualification for deacons as well: "Deacons likewise must be men of dignity" (1 Tim. 3:8). And then in verse 11 he said, "Women must likewise be dignified."

The word literally means "seriousness," in the sense of being "worthy of respect."[5] One commentator said the term "denotes a high moral tone and serious manner."[6] In fact, the King James Version translates the word as "gravity." To be dignified is to have an appropriate sense of gravity or weightiness about you—to be a respectable person who inspires respect.

We need to say what being dignified does *not* mean, so we don't misunderstand this. We don't hear the word often, and it can give the impression of someone who's haughty or condescending—someone who looks down their nose at "those undignified, low-class people."

Neither does the connotation of seriousness or gravity mean a man must always have a dour expression on his face, his brow always furled and his lips always pursed. Dignified does not mean a man is joyless or morose, someone who never smiles or laughs at anything. The dignified man is not that famous (and inaccurate) caricature of the Puritans: someone possessed by "the haunting fear that someone, somewhere, may be happy."

Not at all! The dignified man is happy. He is joyful in the Lord. He enjoys life as a sweet gift from God. He is marked by a grave gladness. The dignified man is glad, but he is grave. He's not goofy, flippant, frivolous, or trivial.

The opposite of gravity is levity. Undignified, immature men are marked by a perpetual levity. Everything is always a joke. They can never let things

5 Knight, *The Pastoral Epistles*, 305.

6 J.N.D. Kelly, *A Commentary on the Pastoral Epistles* (Grand Rapids: Eerdmans, 1981), 242.

get too heavy without injecting some humor. There are some grown men who just refuse to be serious about much of anything. They're just goofy. You couldn't take them seriously if you wanted to, because of the way they carry themselves.

Someone who is constantly joking, always trying to keep things light, seldom willing to have a serious conversation—that's not a mature man who is able to lead, love, provide for, and protect others. That's a little boy who refuses to be exercised about things that matter.

The dignified man is affected by the realities of heaven and hell. He feels as if he's in the presence of heaven, before the face of the omniscient God who searches the heart. And he feels as if the flames of hell were nipping at his feet, reminding him that souls are perishing every day, and that as a preacher of the gospel he traffics in matters of life and death.

The dignified man is awed by the glory of God. In fact, the Hebrew word for "glory" is *chavod,* which actually means heaviness, or weightiness. Nothing about God encourages us to levity. Levity is the enemy of all worship, because worship is a response to the glory, weightiness, and gravity of God's character.

When you meditate on the things of God, when you go before the Lord in prayer and seek to do battle with your own sin, you can't "keep it light," because those are weighty realities. The godly man constantly ruminates on God's Word. He prays at all times without ceasing. He knows his transgressions, and his sin is ever before him (Ps. 51:3). You can't live in the presence of God and be a man of perpetual levity.

Again, I'm not saying you can never laugh or have fun. Not in the least! But the dignified man isn't entertained by the sins that drove Christ to the cross. He doesn't make jokes about sin, and he doesn't sin in order to make jokes. He doesn't make light of vulgarity. One pastor wrote that the dignified man doesn't laugh at what is tragic, and he doesn't laugh at the expense of others.[7] I think that's spot-on.

The dignified man also doesn't seek to draw attention to himself; he does all he can to point attention to Christ. In a real sense, the dignified man seeks to be unremarkable. He doesn't stand out because of his boorishness, or his unfaithfulness to his commitments, or his thirst for attention.

That extends even to his physical appearance. He doesn't present himself as odd or exceptional. He dresses appropriately. He doesn't want his hair, beard, or clothing to be what leaves an impression on people. He wants his

---

7 Chris Mueller, *Let the Men Be Men: God's Design for Manhood and Marriage* (Irvine, CA: Three Sixteen Publishing, 2022), 159.

godliness, patience, graciousness, and edifying speech to leave an impression. He's the kind of person who, after you've spent time with him, you leave thinking less about him and more about the Christ into whose image he is being transformed. We can summarize dignity as "a blend of humility, courtesy, seriousness, and respectfulness."[8]

A Man Is Sound in Doctrine

Another mark of biblical manhood is that he is sound in doctrine. Paul issued this exhortation to both older and younger men. Titus 2:2 says: "Older men are to be temperate, dignified, sensible, sound in faith. . . . " As we mentioned, this is to be sound in *the* faith: that body of doctrine that was once for all delivered to the saints (Jude 1:3). And then Paul said to the young men in Titus 2:7: "Show yourself to be an example of good deeds, with purity in doctrine."

We discussed this when we addressed the man's duty to be a spiritual protector. Men must know theology. In a real sense, we can say that theology is life, because theology is the study of God, and as Jesus said, eternal life is to know God (John 17:3).

Men, nothing in the world is more important than the truth. And we who have turned from our sins and put our faith in the Lord Jesus Christ for salvation—we who claim to be disciples of the One who said, "I am the Truth"—should devote all our energy to searching out the divine mind as He has revealed the truth to us in the Scriptures.

Theology used to be regarded as the queen of the sciences. This meant that the human mind had no higher, nobler, more worthwhile inquiry to be occupied with than the contemplation of God and the glory of His attributes and works. Disciplining our minds and hearts to patiently and faithfully dig through the Word of God in order to accurately and adequately understand who our God is and what He has done for us through Christ is what it means to have a relationship with our God. It is the substance of the Christian life.

Absolutely everything else in your life flows out of that. Everything is downstream of your theology, because everything you do is shaped by what you believe.

This means if you are amiss in your doctrine, you will be amiss in your devotion. If you are wrong in precept, you will be wrong in practice. And you are responsible not only for your own spiritual health, but also for the

8 Mueller, *Let the Men Be Men*, 154.

spiritual health of your wife and children. That means the man must be the resident theologian in the home. He must be able to divide truth from error—to be able "both to exhort in sound doctrine and to refute those who contradict" (Titus 1:9).

God's Word commands men to maintain purity in doctrine, to not let our understanding of the teachings of the Christian faith become polluted with error. That means we must devote ourselves to ever examine our doctrine, subjecting it to the searching light of Scripture, constantly conforming our thoughts to what we see in the text, repenting of our faith in falsehoods, and eagerly embracing the truth.

In First Timothy 4:6, Paul said to Timothy, "In pointing out these things to the brethren, you will be a good servant of Christ Jesus, constantly nourished on the words of the faith and of the sound doctrine which you have been following." Sound doctrine is the nourishment of the child of God. It is the food for your soul, along with the souls of those God gives you to lead.

If you have time for the garage, for the lake, for the shooting range, for the driving range, for the TV, the theater, the cell phone, or whatever—but you don't have time for the *Holiness of God* by R. C. Sproul, for *Strange Fire* by John MacArthur, for *The Glory of Christ* or *The Mortification of Sin* by John Owen, for *A Body of Divinity* by Thomas Watson, for *The Religious Affections* by Jonathan Edwards, and for Augustine and Athanasius and the Gregories and Anselm—you are missing the point of your calling as men.

Men know their God and make their God known to those within their sphere of influence. I don't know of a more fearful thing than to take God's own infallible and inerrant Word about Himself and His world, and to teach error from it—to twist God's own words to say something untrue about Him. For that reason, the biblical man must be sound in doctrine.

A Man Is Sound in Speech

Finally, the biblical man is sound in speech. Paul says in Titus 2:6–8: "Likewise urge the young men to be sensible; in all things show yourself to be an example of good deeds, with purity in doctrine, dignified, sound in speech which is beyond reproach, so that the opponent will be put to shame, having nothing bad to say about us."

No wild beast upon the earth is more difficult to tame than the unglorified, human tongue. James 3:7–8 reads, "Every species of beasts and birds, of reptiles and creatures of the sea, is tamed and has been tamed by the human race. But no one can tame the tongue; it is a restless evil and full of deadly poison." One verse earlier, James said, "And the tongue is a fire, the very world of iniquity."

In fact, "Death and life are in the power of the tongue" (Prov. 18:21), and Jesus said that "every careless word that people speak, they shall give an accounting for it in the day of judgment. For by your words you will be justified, and by your words you will be condemned" (Matt. 12:36–37).

Men—and young men especially—can be careless in speech. But the biblical man must not be. If we will account for every careless word we speak, no wonder Paul instructed Titus to urge men to be sound in speech.

"Sound" is the term *húgiēs,* from which we get the word hygiene. It speaks of healthiness or wholesomeness. "There is one who speaks rashly like the thrusts of a sword," says Proverbs 12:18, "but the tongue of the wise brings healing."

The speech of a biblical man is to be life-giving, the kind of speech that restores spiritual health. This is a way of saying that our words are to be edifying. They are not to tear down, but to build up.

Ephesians 4:29 is absolutely paramount here: "Let no unwholesome word proceed from your mouth, but only such a word as is good for edification according to the need of the moment, so that it will give grace to those who hear."

So few words in just one sentence, and yet so much is to be gleaned from them. Let's consider four types of speech that must not be found in the biblical man's mouth.

No Foul Language

First, we are to use no unwholesome speech. For some strange reason, people think that cutting, profane, vulgar speech is manly. It's not. Movies are sometimes rated "R" for "adult language" or "strong language," based on how much foul language is in them. But that's euphemistic nonsense. Foul language, cursing, and swear words are neither "adult" nor "strong." They are juvenile and weak. A man who cannot speak without cursing sounds like middle school boy. Such a man is so deprived of intelligence and self-discipline that he can't learn to express himself like a sensible, respectable adult. Paul says the biblical man is sound in speech and lets no unwholesome word come out of his mouth.

He added, "There must be no filthiness and silly talk, or coarse jesting, which are not fitting, but rather giving of thanks" (Eph. 5:4). Besides outright foul language, men seem especially prone to the temptation to speak crassly and in sexual innuendo—and then try to excuse it as, "I was only joking" (Prov. 26:19). Paul said that's not fitting. That doesn't match who a Christian is. That doesn't characterize a biblical man. Your speech is to be wholesome, healthy, sound, and hygienic.

No Complaining

Second, not only is your speech to be clean, it should also to be devoid of complaining. I've often said that complaining is the mother tongue of the unregenerate human heart. The native language of sinners is grumbling and grousing. And yet Paul commands us, "Do all things without grumbling or disputing" (Phil. 2:14).

The biblical man must eliminate complaining from his life, because complaining is nothing other than verbalized dissatisfaction with the providence of God. But who are we, mere creatures of the dust, to tell God how to be God? Who are we to tell Him how to providentially order His universe?

Few things are more juvenile and less manly than a guy who sits around and complains about everything. We are to be sound in speech, so our speech is to be free of complaining.

No Gossip

Third, our speaking is to be devoid of gossip. Notice how many times the phrase "malicious gossips" occurs in the pastoral epistles (1 Tim. 3:11; 5:13; 2 Tim. 3:3; Titus 2:3). Note that phrase translates the Greek word *diabolos,* which is the same word for "devil."

We'll say more about gossip when we address biblical womanhood, but the bottom line is: Men don't spend time like idle busybodies, whispering about other people's business—especially if it has the potential to destroy other people's reputations. If it's not true, necessary to be said, kind, and your business, don't speak it, and don't listen to it.[9]

No Lies

Finally, our speech is to be devoid of lies. Ephesians 4:25 commands: "Therefore, laying aside falsehood, 'speak truth each one of you with his neighbor,' for we are members of one another." Colossians 3:9 adds: "Do not lie to one another, since you laid aside the old self with its evil practices."

Lying is unacceptable for the man of God. Why? Because he has been saved by a Savior who is Himself the Truth (John 14:6). We have been saved by the word of truth (Col. 1:5). We owe our lives to the truth. We should be walking expositions of the truth!

9 Mueller, *Let the Men Be Men*, 177.

I can hardly think of anything more incongruent than a Christian whose word cannot be depended upon to reflect truth. A biblical man's word is trustworthy. What he says is dependable. It is not crafted to deceive, nor full of exaggeration and hyperbole such that it could mislead those who take his words at face value. It is "the open statement of the truth" (2 Cor. 4:2).

A man gives his word, and it stands inviolable. His yes is yes (Matt. 5:37; 2 Cor. 1:17–20; James 5:12), and he does not go back on his word. Even if he swears to his own hurt, he does not change (Ps. 15:4). To be sound in speech is to speak as a faithful witness to the truth.

In everything, the biblical man asks, "Will this build up? Will this give grace? Are these words necessary at this time?"

Few things transform our speech more than meditating on the standard set in Ephesians 4:29. We should only speak if our speech will edify, if it will give grace, and if the moment calls for it.

A Summary of Biblical Manhood

Here we are again, humbled to the dust before the standard of God's Word. The biblical man is a leader, a lover, a provider, and a protector. He is strong, sensible, dignified, sound in doctrine, and sound in speech.

Young men, this is what you must aspire to be. Older men, this is what you must model. Single women, this is what you must seek in a husband. Wives, this is what you are to help your husband be. To all, this is what you must pray the men of our churches would become.

Despite how far short we fall (and we do), let us press on by the grace of Christ to walk in the fullness of the power of what He has purchased for us. This is what Almighty God has created us to be, in fulfillment of His very good design for us as His creatures.

Many of us within the church are quick to protest against the wickedness of the homosexualist and transgender movements, and rightly so. But men, those protestations amount to little if you will not put your own hand to the plow of living out your calling as biblical men. It does little good to shout from the rooftops that men are not women if you don't try to be the kind of man that Scripture calls you to be. I pray these chapters will awaken your conscience from its slumber and set you to action.

But we do grieve at how far short we fall in some of these areas. That grief is good. Godly sorrow works repentance. But it does not work despair (2 Cor. 7:9–10). If you feel defeated by how far short you fall from this standard, remember the Man Christ Jesus (1 Tim. 2:5). He is your perfect example. How gracious of God to show us the perfect Man, the perfect image of God—holiness in our own nature!

- He is the great head of the church, who takes responsibility for the bride He leads.
- He is love incarnate, who lays down His life in sacrifice for our good.
- He is the great provider, who nourishes us and cherishes us with the spiritual food that saves and sustains the soul.
- He is the foremost protector, who steps in between us and our Judge and bears the awful, wrath-filled punishment in our place. Once in His hand, none can be snatched out.
- He is the strongest man to ever live, living His entire life as strength under control, wielded only for the benefit of others.
- He is not just sensible, but also the wisdom of God incarnate; always self-controlled.
- He is dignified—the gravest Man ever to walk the earth, the Man *of* Sorrows, as if He were made up only of sorrows, because He saw how people so carelessly forfeit the joys of heaven and cling to the miseries of sin and hell.
- He is the Great Prophet, the Teacher of only sound doctrine.
- And He is the Word of God Himself, always sound in speech, to the point that the people wondered at the words of grace that fell from His lips.

He is everything we must be!

Because of that, He is not merely our example; He is our substitute. Christ doesn't come just to show us how to live; He comes to show us how we've failed to live, and then He lives for us! Jesus obeys the law in our place, so that, not only does His death pay our penalty, but His life accomplishes our righteousness (Matt. 3:15; Rom. 5:18–19).

For all who are humbled by this standard of manhood, who are tempted to despair because of how faithless you can be, raise your eyes to the cross of Calvary and see Him there, who made an end of all your sin. Behold Him there, the Risen Lamb, your perfect, spotless righteousness. Looking away from yourself, and trusting entirely in Him, fall on His grace to be for you what you could not be in yourself. Receive the perfect robe of His righteousness that makes you stand in the presence of Holy God.

And then, having feasted on that gospel, walk in the strength of that gospel. Apply the grace that purchases your pardon unto the power of holy living. Taste how gracious Jesus is with you in the gospel and then in His day-to-day dealings with you as you walk with Him. Then, bend that grace out horizontally to others to lead, love, provide, and protect; to be strong, sensible, dignified, and sound in doctrine and speech.

You can be this man, brothers. Christ has purchased grace for you to do it. God has prepared these good works that you would walk in them. Give yourselves to your wives, to your children, to your brothers and sisters in Christ, so Christ will get what He's worthy of from you.

Study Questions:

1. Is it a biblical requirement for a man to be physically strong? Support your answer with Scripture. Do you meet the standard Scripture sets? If not, how will you make progress?

2. What is the difference between meekness and weakness? How do you see traits of each in yourself? What do you need to do about that?

3. What is your orientation toward conflict? Are you too quick to engage or too quick to flee? What practical steps can you take to improve?

4. When was the last time someone brought you biblical correction? When was the last time you accepted biblical correction without arguing? What can you do to invite correction from mature believers?

5. What attribute of sensibility do you struggle with most? What strategies will you implement to put off that sin and put on righteousness in its place?

6. Would you characterize yourself as a dignified man? Why or why not? How can you grow in both gravity and gladness?

7. What steps will you take in the next three months to sharpen your understanding of sound biblical doctrine?

8. The chapter mentioned foul language, complaining, gossip, and lying as types of speech that fall short of God's standard. Which of those is the greatest challenge for you? What practical steps will you take to mortify that sin?

10

Handcrafted to Help

The Beauty of Biblical Submission

IN 2022, THE POPULAR conservative commentator, Matt Walsh, of *The Daily Wire*, released a documentary entitled *What is a Woman?* In it, he traveled the world, interviewing people and asking that very question: "What is a woman?"

Just a few years ago, that would have been a very short film! But the twisted moment in which we find ourselves as a culture has made that question one of profound philosophical import. Shockingly, hardly anyone Walsh spoke to could give a straight answer. "Are you a woman?" "Yes, I identify as a woman." "Ok. What is that?" Blank stare. He followed up, "When you say you identify as a woman, what is that thing, specifically, that you're identifying as?"

People all over the country said they didn't know and walked away. "Do you identify as a woman?" "Yes I do." "What is a woman?" "I don't know."

Now, we find that ridiculous. And we should. But can you, as the people of God, answer Walsh's question any better?

Surely, yes, in one sense, we can answer rightly: A woman is an adult human female. But if we asked, "What does it mean to behave like a woman?" could we give the Bible's answer?

What is femininity, according to God's Word? What has our Creator designed a woman to be? If we reject transgenderism for the delusion that it is and recognize that women should look and speak and behave like women and not men, can we explain from Scripture what it means to be a woman and not a man?

These questions cause us within the church to eschew unbiblical, worldly notions of masculinity and femininity and to press toward the Bible's teaching on the characteristics of biblical manhood and womanhood. Having searched out the marks of biblical masculinity, we come now to discern Scripture's teaching on biblical femininity.

A Reminder on Singleness and Marriage

At the outset, it's important to reiterate that the Bible's description of genuine womanhood often relates to how a wife interacts with her husband. And that is just because marriage is indeed the norm for mankind. Remember, as soon as we read of "male and female" in Genesis 1:27, we hear about being fruitful and multiplying in Genesis 1:28. As soon as we learn that woman is man's suitable helper in Genesis 2:22–23, we hear about the two becoming one flesh in Genesis 2:24. While God has not ordained that every person would be married, it is nevertheless His general, normal design for His image-bearers. Because of that, much of Scripture's teaching on masculinity and femininity speaks to how we conduct ourselves toward a spouse or how we are to prepare ourselves for that relationship.

But as we said concerning manhood, that doesn't mean a woman is less of a woman if she is not married. Being single puts you at no more disadvantage to living out the calling of your womanhood than Jesus' singleness put Him at a disadvantage to living out the calling of His manhood. Single women can practice biblical, appropriate expressions of femininity even toward the men in their lives who are not their husbands.

Just as we discovered nine marks of biblical manhood, we find the Scripture also reveals at least nine marks of biblical womanhood. They describe what a Christian woman should aspire to be as she seeks to live according to God's Word. They outline what kind of woman godly young men should pursue as a potential wife.

These nine marks are not weapons for husbands to use to complain about how their wives don't measure up, but tools that will help husbands pray for their wives and labor for their wives' spiritual growth, as they serve their wives' sanctification (Eph. 5:26).

A Suitable Helper

The first mark of biblical womanhood is that a woman is created to be a helper—a mark of the woman's identity that we find at the inception of her creation. After God created the man, placed him in the garden, and gave him His law, "*Then* Yahweh God said, 'It is not good for the man to be alone; I will make a helper suitable for him'" (Gen. 2:18).

Throughout the first chapter of the creation account, we see the refrain, "And God saw that it was good" (1:10, 12, 18, 21, 25, 31). Into chapter two, every tree was "good for food" (2:9), and "the gold of [the] land is good" (2:12). But suddenly, verse 18 arrests us with the declaration that something about the Paradise of Eden was not good. It was not good that the man had no helper.

So, God brought every animal to the man to be named. But of all those creatures, "For Adam there was not found a helper suitable for him" (2:20). None corresponded to him as his equal and counterpart. Then, God put the man to sleep, took a rib from his side, and made the helper suitable for Adam: the woman (2:21–22).

I'm not sure a greater honor can be bestowed upon women than to realize that God Himself declared that His own perfectly created Paradise was not good until the woman was created to complement the man. Women are not unimportant, second-class, or inferior. Women are so essential that Paradise itself was in a sense incomplete without her.

Certainly man is incomplete without her; he needs someone to be a helper suitable for him in the way no other creature is—someone who will bring unique gifts, talents, and strengths to the human race that will enable mankind to glorify their God in obedience to His commands.

We can't miss this. God's design in creating the woman was that she would be a helper, suitable for the man to carry out the divine mandate given in Genesis 1:28: "Be fruitful and multiply, and fill the earth." Thus, the foundation of what it means to be woman is to be one who can suitably help a man walk in obedience to the calling that God has placed on his life.

The Beauty of Joyful Submission

And that helpfulness—the wife's putting herself at the disposal of her husband, yielding her gifts and strengths to his benefit—is at the heart of what Scripture often refers to as submission. This submission complements the man's headship in beautiful, glorious harmony: two image-bearers, equal in status and dignity before God, but with distinct roles. The husband leads, and the wife helps; the husband initiates, and the wife responds in submission to the husband's leadership.

When we spoke about biblical leadership, we observed that its heart was not license or lordship, but responsibility. Leadership is a stewardship to lead in a way that honors God and benefits those under a one's charge. A biblical man takes responsibility, eschews passivity, and provides a pattern of initiative.[1] Corresponding to that, a biblical woman submissively responds to the pattern of initiatives established by mature masculinity in a way that honors and affirms (rather than usurps or challenges) his leadership.[2]

Now, in a culture dominated by expressive individualism, in which the chief virtue is to vent every thought and desire you've ever had—where fighting your basest impulses is derided as inauthenticity—submission has been turned into a four-letter word. But Christians should have no problem with the concept of submission. Our entire worldview is grounded upon submission to the Lordship of Jesus (Matt. 28:18; Rom. 10:9; 1 Cor. 12:3; Eph. 1:19–23).

We're not singling out wives; we want everyone to be brought into willing subjection to the will of God. Further, citizens submit to the governing authorities in the civil sphere (Rom. 13:1). Church members submit to elders in the ecclesiastical sphere (Heb. 13:17). Children obey their parents in the familial sphere (Eph. 6:1). In the same way, according to Christ's own directives for life in His church, wives are to submit to their husbands (Eph. 5:22; Col. 3:18).

What does this joyful submission—this happy helpfulness—look like? What characterizes it? Scripture outlines no fewer than nine features of biblical submission.

ITS DIVINE DESIGN

First, this beautiful harmony of the roles of male headship and female submission was the divine design of our holy, sovereign, and wise God from the beginning of creation. We've seen that already in Genesis 2:18, which speaks of woman being created to be a helper before the corruption of sin entered the world. But we also see it in the categorical statements of the New Testament. Paul instructed,

> Wives, be subject to your own husbands, as to the Lord. For the husband is the head of the wife, as Christ also is the head of the church, He Himself being the Savior of the body. But as the church is subject to Christ, so also the wives ought to be to their husbands in everything. (Eph. 5:22–24)

In First Corinthians 11:3, he spoke even more broadly than the husband-wife relationship: "But I want you to understand that Christ is the head of every man, and the man is the head of a woman." A few verses later, he added, "For indeed man was not created for the woman's sake, but woman for the man's sake" (1 Cor. 11:9). God created the woman for the man, to be his helper.

1 Piper, *What's the Difference?*, 31.

2 Piper, *What's the Difference?*, 49.

The divine design of submission is evident even in man's fall. Mankind's first sin consisted in the man's abdication and the woman's usurpation of male headship. God addressed the man first and commanded him to not eat from the tree before Eve was even created, which was one of many indications of man's headship in the garden. But Satan arrived, and "he said to the *woman*, 'Indeed, has God said . . . '" (Gen. 3:1).

The serpent put his craftiness on display (Gen. 3:4) when he spoke to the woman first, making Eve the one who spoke on behalf of the family (Gen. 3:2), as if he were tempting her, "You decide, Eve! You lead the way!"[3]

This was an immediate, subtle subversion of the very good created order of God, defined in the loving headship and sweet submission of man and woman in marriage. It's remarkable that mankind's fall into sin was an occasion of contravening the divine design of headship and submission. How fundamental to the identity of man and woman must these realities be!

These texts, along with the many others we considered in the chapters on manhood, communicate the truth of the complementary roles of male headship and female submission. Because these roles originated with the creation of man and woman, they do not have their origin in the fall, as is so often alleged. They are not the result of sin's corruption of our relationships but are rooted in God's very-good design. Fundamental to the identity of man and woman, from the very beginning of their existence, before their corruption and fall into sin, is that the biblical man is a leader, and the biblical woman is a helper.

Its Cursed Difficulty

Secondly, consider the cursed difficulty of submission. Since submission is God's design for the woman from her creation, why is it typically so difficult for women to embrace that role?

And it *is* difficult. Men struggle to embrace their role of loving, sacrificial headship; they either passively neglect responsibility or cruelly assert authority. In a similar way, women struggle mightily with the temptation to seize the role of leadership for themselves and exercise authority over men. Why is that such a common thread in human relationships, when God created us to do just the opposite?

It's because we have fallen from that state of blessedness in which God originally created mankind. In fact, Genesis 3:17 tells us that it is because Adam "listened to the voice of [his] wife"—precisely because he abdicated

3 Ortlund, "Male-Female Equality and Male Headship," 108.

his leadership and submitted to Eve's leadership—that the curse of God came upon the serpent, the woman, the man, and the creation itself. We read of the curse of God upon the woman: "To the woman [God] said, 'I will greatly multiply Your pain in childbirth, In pain you will bring forth children.'" Then notice this phrase: "Your desire will be for your husband, [but] he will rule over you" (Gen. 3:16).

Those same two words—*teshuqah,* "desire," and *māshal,* "to rule," or "to master"—appear in Genesis 4:7, and the context of that passage helps us make sense of this one.

In Genesis 4, Cain's countenance had fallen because God had no regard for his offering, and God responded to Cain's anger and sadness by urging him to battle temptation: "And if you do not do well, sin is crouching at the door; and its desire is for you *[teshuqah]*, but you must rule over it *[māshal]*." God was saying that sin is like a roaring animal, waiting to strike Cain at the proper time. Sin's desire was to exert mastery over Cain, to rule him, to reign in his life; and if he passively refused to withstand it, it would overtake him. Instead of that, the Lord exhorted Cain to rule over sin. He said Cain must exert mastery over sin.

If we apply the sense of "desire" and "rule" gleaned from Genesis 4:7 to the interpretation of the same terms back in Genesis 3:16, the meaning becomes clear. Part of the curse on Eve is that a woman will want to exert mastery over her husband—to rule over him the way sin wanted to rule over Cain. Instead of man yielding to woman's desire, he will withstand it in the same way that Cain should have resisted sin's desire to reign over him.

While God had designed the beauty of headship and submission to sing together in glorious, peaceful harmony, the curse of dissonance and conflict would reign in the relationship between man and woman. One commentator writes, "God gives the woman up to a desire to have her way with her husband. Because she usurped his headship in the temptation, God hands her over to the misery of competition with her rightful head."[4]

Therefore, we may say, without irony or sarcasm, that the feminist movement is satanic. The philosophy and worldview of second- and third-wave feminism seduces women into eschewing submission and casting off the role of helper, and into seizing authority and asserting their dominance.

Feminism confuses equal rights with identical roles. In so doing, feminism is nothing more than the recitation of the tempter's deception of the first woman.

---

4 Ortlund, "Male-Female Equality and Male Headship," 109.

So, I say to my sisters in Christ, your inclination, which seems almost natural to buck against the loving authority of your husband, is not a trifling matter. To reject the glorious, beautiful role of submission that God has ordained for you is to follow in the footsteps of Eve in committing the sin that plunged the human race into condemnation. It is to live consistently with and yield to the curse of sin that plagues the entire creation.

If you would live in a godly way, consistent with the blessedness of Genesis 1 and 2 rather than consistent with the curse of Genesis 3, you will resist sin's mastery over you, and therefore, resist your inclination to usurp headship over your husband.

Its Gospel-Shaped Motive

Thirdly, consider the gospel-shaped motive of submission, which we find once again in Ephesians 5:22–24: "Wives, be subject to your own husbands, as to the Lord. For the husband is the head of the wife, as Christ also is the head of the church, He Himself being the Savior of the body. But as the church is subject to Christ, so also the wives ought to be to their husbands in everything."

In this text, Paul called upon wives to submit to their own husbands "as to the Lord."

Now, the term "as" expresses similarity, not identity. Paul did not teach that a husband is the lord over his wife in the same way that Christ is Lord over them both. Christ's authority is absolute; a husband's is not. Christ is a perfectly sinless leader who never needs to ask forgiveness and is always worthy of our trust. A husband is not.

Nevertheless, while the term doesn't communicate identity, it does communicate similarity. A wife ought to be voluntarily yielding to her husband in love in a way similar to how she voluntarily yields to the Lord Jesus in love. Because it is ultimately the command of the Triune God for wives to submit to their husbands, a wife's submission to her husband *is* her submitting to the Lord. Conversely, a wife's rebellion against her husband's legitimate authority is rebellion against the Lord Jesus.

We also notice that nothing in the passage makes the command for wifely submission contingent upon the husband deserving that submission. The text doesn't say a wife is to submit to her husband only when he does his part to love his wife like Christ loved the church—not any more than it says that a husband should love his wife as Christ loves the church only when she submits to him as the church does to Christ.

That, of course, is the ideal. And when it happens, the beauty of biblical complementarity is on display for all to see: The husband gives his life away to lovingly and sacrificially provide for and protect his wife; and the wife gives her life away in joyful, eager submission to her husband's leadership.

But the standard for a wife's submission is not relaxed when her husband fails to love her well, because the apostle Peter issued this same call for wives to be submissive even to their husbands who are unbelievers (1 Pet. 3:1–2). Wives are called to submit to their husbands even when the husbands don't deserve it.

Why? Because God designed loving headship and joyful submission in marriage to be a picture of the gospel—of the covenant-keeping grace of Jesus Christ toward His bride, the church.

Paul said the husband pictures Christ and the wife pictures the church. When a wife submits to her husband's leadership, she displays to the world what a joy it is for the church of Jesus Christ to submit to the leadership of her Lord. When she follows her husband's leadership with the gentle and quiet spirit of a respectful and supportive wife, she preaches to the watching world that Christ is so glorious and satisfying that His bride, the church, is happy to follow Him anywhere.

This gospel-shaped motive sweetens the duty of submission into a delight. Is it not a joy for you, ladies, as members of the bride of Christ, to submit to Christ your bridegroom? Is He not a loving leader? Is He not full of wisdom to lead you into paths of righteousness and blessing? Is He not worthy of the joyful, eager submission of every person in the world?

Of course He is! Paul said when you submit to your own husband, you display that truth to the world. And so that is a source of strength to fight the temptation to rebel.

When it's difficult to follow your husband, when he is proving unworthy of your submission, ask yourself if Jesus is worthy of your submission. Ask yourself if Jesus is worthy of His church's submission. There, you'll find the gloriously feminine strength to obey Christ and to walk in wifely submission.

Its Pervasive Extent

In the fourth place, we must briefly comment on the pervasive extent of submission. Paul called wives to be subject to their husbands "in everything" (Eph. 5:24). This means all we have talked about concerning submission applies to every area of life. Some have contended that Paul's call to wifely submission is to be read as extending only to certain wifely duties. But the pervasiveness of the phrase "in everything" won't allow for a narrow view of submission. Just as there is no aspect of the church's life that she may reserve from the Lordship of Christ, neither is there any aspect of a wife's life that she may reserve from her husband's authority.

Its Biblical Limits

Having said that, though, we must observe the limits of biblical submission. The call to submit "in everything" does not rule out any limitations whatsoever. But it *doesn't* mean, as Charles Hodge explains, that

> the wife is . . . subject as to some things, and independent as to others . . . [neither] does [it] mean that the authority of the husband is unlimited. It teaches its extent, not its degree. It extends over all departments, but is limited in all—first, by the nature of the relation; and, secondly, by the higher authority of God.[5]

So, by calling a wife to submit to her husband in everything, Paul did not mean to include those thoughts, attitudes, and behaviors that are sinful. A wife must not follow her husband's leadership into sin.[6] That should go without saying, but we must say it.

We see that same pattern when Paul calls for Christian submission to the government in the civil sphere. In Romans 13, Paul called for "every person . . . to be in subjection to the governing authorities," and he included no qualification. However, if civil authority commands a believer to disobey God, the believer's response must be what Peter and the apostles answered the high priest: "We must obey God rather than men" (Acts 5:29). Paul himself defied the governing authorities when he disobeyed the chief magistrates' orders to leave the jail in Philippi (Acts 16:35–40). Thus, even where there is an unqualified command for pervasive submission, that does not give license to any Christian under any form of authority to follow their authority into sin.

This means a wife not only may, but must, refuse to submit to her husband if he demands that she do something that God forbids—like engage in deception or dishonesty, or get drunk with him, or watch pornography

---

5 Charles Hodge, *Ephesians*, Geneva Series of Commentaries (Carlisle, PA: Banner of Truth, 2003), 230.

6 Piper, *What's the Difference?*, 52.

with him, or engage in any sort of illegal activity.[7] Similarly, she must refuse to follow his leadership if he forbids her to do something God commands—like read her Bible, or go to church, or evangelize. She will have to say "no" to that kind of headship, because the authority of Christ over her life supersedes the authority of her husband.

However, even when a wife must obey God rather than her husband, she must still express her inability to follow him in a spirit of submission, rather than in a spirit of rancor and rebellion.

She could say, "I'm not doing that! And it's disgusting that you would ask me to!" But instead of using the opportunity to demean her husband's authority and rejoice in her disobedience to him, she should speak to him in a way that shows she's grieved that she has to disobey him. She can express that he is making her choose between submitting to him, which ordinarily she loves to do, and obeying Christ, which she also loves to do and must do above all else.

One writer gave voice to that kind of submissive disobedience like this. A wife could say, "It grieves me when you venture into sinful acts and want to take me with you. You know I can't do that. I have no desire to resist you. On the contrary, I flourish most when I can respond joyfully to your lead; but I can't follow you into sin, as much as I love to honor your leadership in our marriage. Christ is my King."[8]

That kind of respectful attitude shows the disposition of submission, even where particular acts of submission are not permitted.

Further, a wife is not called to submit herself to being physically or sexually abused by her husband. If a husband so perverts the authority he's been given to protect his wife into harming and even abusing his wife, so that her physical safety is legitimately in danger, she is under no obligation to just sit there and take it. That is not what biblical submission means. Where there is imminent danger, she needs to call the police, notify the elders of her church, and get to a place where she is safe. That may mean that a temporary separation is warranted. It may even mean that divorce is permissible, though that would depend on the details in each case and would need to be worked through under the oversight of her elders. But in no way is she under any biblical warrant to subject herself to physical harm.

A third limit to biblical submission is that Scripture limits a wife's submission to her own husband. The Bible does not teach that all women are to

7 Piper, *What's the Difference?*, 52.

8 Piper, *This Momentary Marriage*, 102.

submit to all men, except perhaps in the sense that all Christians are to "be subject to one another in the fear of Christ" (Eph. 5:21).

Instead, Scripture explicitly calls wives to submit to their own husbands: "Wives, be subject to your own husbands, as to the Lord" (Eph. 5:22); "being subject to their own husbands, so that the word of God will not be dishonored" (Titus 2:5); "In the same way, you wives, be submissive to your own husbands" (1 Pet. 3:1). Pastor John MacArthur put it memorably when he said, "Women, as a group, are not made serfs to men in general, and men aren't automatically elevated to a ruling class over all women."[9]

At the same time, that isn't to say that the only arena for a woman's submissiveness is in marriage. Just as there are appropriate ways for a biblical man to express his responsibility to lead, provide for, and protect women who are not his wife, there are also appropriate ways for a biblical woman to express her responsibility to affirm and nurture those expressions of worthy, biblical masculinity.

There is a submissiveness that marks a woman's character in a general sense, even beyond the husband-wife relationship. Though she is not to submit to all men in the same sense that she would submit to her husband, she should have that prevailing disposition of affirming and supporting godly male headship wherever it is encountered.

We see that, for example, in First Timothy 2:11. In that letter, Paul instructed the church at Ephesus how to conduct themselves as the Lord's church—what life in the household of God was to be like. Paul said, "A woman must quietly receive instruction with entire submissiveness." That is not because a woman is inferior to a man; she is not. It is not because she may not be gifted to teach; many women are. It is simply because the design of God, rooted in His created order, is that equal image-bearers function in distinct but harmonious roles to the praise of His glory. This passage teaches that this extends not only to the home but also to the church. The prevailing disposition of a biblical woman is to affirm worthy male headship in ways appropriate to her varying relationships.[10]

So, if a young man's responsibility to be a provider leads him to pay for his date's meal or movie ticket or walk his friend to her car to ensure her safety, mature femininity isn't offended by those things, as if they were an attack

9 John MacArthur, "The Submissive Wife," www.gty.org/library/blog/B100825 (accessed December 2023).

10 Piper, *What's the Difference?*, 89.

on her independence. She gratefully, and humbly receives those gentlemanly courtesies as appropriate expressions of masculine provision and protection.

ITS PRACTICAL OUTWORKING

In that vein, then, consider the practical outworking of submission. The term itself, used in all the passages we've quoted (Eph. 5; Col. 3; Titus 2; 1 Pet. 3), is the Greek word *hupotassō.* It means to place oneself under another. It is the idea of putting yourself at the disposal of someone else—yielding your desires, your will, your abilities, and your efforts to serve and benefit another. This is precisely what it means to be a helper, which Genesis 2:18 identifies as fundamental to a woman's identity.

Therefore, as we said before, the foundation of what it means to be woman is to be one who can suitably help a man to walk in obedience to the calling that God has placed on his life, by placing herself at the disposal of her husband's leadership, yielding her gifts and strengths unto his benefit. Submission is a biblical woman's response to the pattern of initiatives established by mature masculinity in a way that honors and affirms (rather than usurps or challenges) his leadership.[11]

In their excellent book, *Recovering Biblical Manhood and Womanhood,* John Piper and Wayne Grudem put it this way: "Submission refers to a wife's divine calling to honor and affirm her husband's leadership and help carry it through according to her gifts."[12] Elsewhere, Piper explained,

> A mature woman is glad when a respectful, caring, upright man offers sensitive strength and provides a pattern of appropriate initiatives in their relationship. She does not want to reverse these roles. She is glad when he is not passive. She feels herself enhanced and honored and freed by his caring strength and servant-leadership.[13]

In terms of practical outworking, a submissive wife uses her unique gifts and strengths to make her husband the best leader he can be. If mature masculinity takes the initiative to be the spiritual leader, mature femininity:

- actively supports their family's meaningful (and punctual) participation in their local church;

---

11 Piper, *What's the Difference?*, 49.

12 John Piper and Wayne Grudem, "An Overview of Central Concerns: Questions and Answers," in *Recovering Biblical Manhood and Womanhood*, 61.

13 Piper, *What's the Difference?*, 56.

- eagerly participates in family devotions, Bible reading, and prayer together;
- responds enthusiastically to her husband's suggestions about books to read or sermons to listen to together;
- engages undistractedly in spiritual conversations;
- invites her husband's spiritual oversight and humbly receives the correction he might bring;
- happily encourages him with words of kindness when he leads, protects, and provides for her well, and when he makes discernible progress in his own sanctification;
- genuinely seeks his input on how to address behavioral issues with the children, and comes alongside him in implementing God-honoring discipline;
- disciplines her own heart in the midst of conflict, so if he outdoes her in showing honor and seeks forgiveness first, her heart is eager and ready to grant it, as well as to seek forgiveness for her part;
- defers with enthusiasm to his suggestions for date nights, family vacations, or fun weekend activities;
- readily offers her prayerful and thoughtful input on any decisions that he brings to her for consideration;
- and, if after patient discussion and prayer, a husband and wife disagree over the direction to take the family (as long as the choice isn't between sin and righteousness, but the wisest of two lawful alternatives), submission means the wife will humbly yield to her husband's leadership and affirm his decision, knowing God will hold him accountable for the rightness or wrongness of the decision, but He will hold her accountable for submitting to the authority that He has placed over her.[14]

None of that means submission is shutting off your brain and mindlessly agreeing with everything your husband says. It can't mean that, because in the same breath that Peter called wives to submit to their husbands, he said they might win their husbands to faith in the gospel by their chaste and respectful behavior (1 Pet. 3:1–2).

14 As an aside, men: good leaders don't pull rank like that as a habit. If you're often calling your wife to submit to you amid unresolved disagreement, something is amiss, and it's likely that you're not leading well. Good leaders *lead*; they do not *drive*.

A submissive wife can't mindlessly agree with her unbelieving husband in everything. So, submission doesn't mean that a woman doesn't have her own thoughts and opinions. It means she will employ those thoughts and opinions in the service of her husband's leadership.

It doesn't mean that you acquiesce to every word your husband says. That wouldn't serve him well, and you are given to him to help him. It simply means that you place your gifts and talents at his disposal to make him the best leader he can be and to follow him in the decisions he makes and the direction he chooses for your family.

Neither is it to say that a wife can't appeal to her husband to change his mind about a decision. She can. But the way she expresses her concern should communicate that, though she doesn't agree, she endorses his leadership and affirms his role as her head.

For example, if he wants to invest a sizeable portion of the family's savings in a venture she doesn't feel comfortable with, she could say, "Nope! You're not doing it! We're equal partners in this marriage. That is my money too, and I won't let you bankrupt this family with your foolishness!"

Or, she can say, "Hey, I know you've thought a lot about this, and I'm thankful that you're taking the initiative to plan for our future and care for us financially, and I know we've talked a lot about it, too. But I still can't shake this feeling of uneasiness, and I'd really like to talk about it again before we move forward. Could we set aside some time to do that?"

The difference in those responses speaks volumes about the state of a woman's heart. The former response belittles, demeans, and usurps headship. The latter encourages, edifies, and honors headship.

Its Respectful Posture

That leads to a seventh feature, namely, the respectful posture of submission. As Paul brought the most extended New Testament instruction on marriage to a climax, he said, "Each individual among you also is to love his own wife even as himself, and the wife must see to it that she respects her husband" (Eph. 5:33).

The conclusion he wanted ringing in Christians' ears was: Husbands, love your wives as yourself; and wives, respect your husbands. Similarly, Peter urged wives to submit even to unbelieving husbands, in the hopes that their gracious behavior would win their disobedient husbands to the truth: "In the same way, you wives, be submissive to your own husbands so that even if any of them are disobedient to the word, they may be won without a word by the behavior of their wives, as they observe your chaste and respectful behavior" (1 Pet. 3:1–2).

That really is an astounding passage. Peter wrote that a biblical wife will win over her disobedient, unbelieving husband—not by confronting him, not by arguing with him, not by nagging him or badgering him or needling him, but by respecting him. She will win him by being a living monument to the truth she professes to believe; by demonstrating in actions that the grace of Christ is powerful to subdue sin.

She will show that grace has empowered her to mortify that self-righteous, unmerciful, speck-picking spirit that constantly finds fault. She will show that grace has empowered her to put on a life of encouraging words that build up instead of tear down, of kind service that never returns evil for evil, and of an attitude and demeanor of respect.

One of the greatest gifts a wife can give her husband is the sure and certain confidence that he has her respect—to know that she trusts him, and that he makes her feel safe as he leads their family.

You say, "But what if he doesn't lead my family? How can I be submissive and responsive to my husband's leadership if he doesn't lead?"

Well, that certainly is a trial. My first plea is: Men, don't give your wife a reason to make this objection! But ladies, the way to help a man embrace his role as leader is not to usurp his leadership by complaining and being contentious. You don't communicate that you desire to follow him by haranguing him to be a better leader. In that case, you would be leading him; and you'd be doing a bad job of it, because nagging and haranguing is not good leadership.

Instead, your pleas for godlier leadership have to sound like, "I want you to be all that God calls you to be, so that we can all experience the fullness of His blessing." It cannot sound like, "I just can't stand you until you change!"

You can say, "Honey, it is a delight for me to follow your leadership. The great longing of my heart is to follow you as you follow Christ. I really desire to place my own giftedness at your disposal in order to maximize divine blessing in our lives. And one area where I would love to see us make progress is [fill in the blank]." That communicates that you're on the same team, that you're in his corner, and that you're ready to follow where he leads.

ITS BEAUTIFUL ATTITUDE

The eighth feature of biblical submission is closely related to that: the beautiful attitude of submission. This will be a main point of our next chapter, so I'll mention it only briefly. We find the beautiful attitude of submission in First Peter 3:3–4: "Your adornment must not be merely external—braiding the hair, and wearing gold jewelry, or putting on dresses; but let it be the hidden person of the heart, with the imperishable quality of a gentle and quiet spirit, which is precious in the sight of God."

A submissive woman is not abrasive or loud. She is gentle and quiet. Her character, attitude, demeanor, and speech are marked by the inward, imperishable beauty of gentleness and quietness. More to come on that in chapter 11.

ITS BEAUTIFYING PURPOSE

Finally, consider the beautifying purpose of submission. We see it in Titus 2:5, where Paul instructed the older women to teach the younger women to be "subject to their own husbands, so that the word of God will not be dishonored."

The Word of God is so filled with the truths of male headship and female submission—those truths are so integral to the very design of God in His creative purposes—that for a professing Christian woman to not be subject to her own husband would be to bring dishonor upon the Word that she professes to believe in.

When any Christian proclaims that the grace of Christ is powerful to transform lives but then does not live that transformed life, it gives cause for the unbeliever to revile. "Some sanctifying word you have! You say the Bible is true and authoritative and lovely and powerful. Why don't you do what it says? You talk a big game, but the Bible says you're supposed to submit yourself to your husband, to be chaste and respectful, to be gentle and quiet, and you run roughshod over him more than I do my own husband!" That is the kind of dishonor a disobedient Christian brings upon the Word of God.

On the other hand, just a few verses later, Paul urged Christian slaves to be subject to their masters "so that they will adorn the doctrine of God our Savior in every respect" (Titus 2:10).

What he expressed negatively in verse 5—that the Word not be dishonored—he expressed positively in verse 10: that the doctrine of God would be adorned. The Greek term is *kosméō,* from which we get the term cosmetics. It means to beautify.

Paul was saying that when a woman cultivates a disposition of free, glad, willing submissiveness, rather than dishonoring the Word of God and making it look less glorious than it is, she adorns the doctrine of God. She beautifies it. She makes it look as glorious as it actually is.

Dear sister, which do you want to be marked by? Isn't it glorious to think that there's something we can do to make the precious Word of God look beautiful in the eyes of believers and unbelievers alike?

Let that thought, along with all we've spoken in this chapter, strengthen your resolve to live your life in that distinctively feminine way, of cultivating the beautiful disposition of glad submissiveness.

A Perfect Example

And if you lack motivation for that, sisters, look to your Savior. No one has ever been more submissive than the Lord of all creation. Though existing in the very nature of God, unencumbered by the limitations of a human existence, existing in a state of equality with God the Father, and enjoying the uninterrupted worship of the saints and angels in heaven, He emptied Himself (Phil. 2:6–7). He took on the nature of finite humanity, and experienced the limitations of hunger, thirst, and weariness. Though He was the eternal lawgiver, He took on a human nature whereby He would submit to His Father's loving rule, and would yield Himself to unjust arrest, to corrupted justice, to false accusations, to beatings, and even to execution as if He were a common criminal. He submitted Himself in this way to secure your redemption, to forgive the very sins which cause you to struggle to bring yourself into submission to the authorities He's placed in your life. Consider Him. Look upon that One with the eyes of faith.

If you will conduct yourselves in a manner worthy of the gospel (Phil. 1:27), if you will walk worthy of the God who calls you into His kingdom and glory (1 Thess. 2:12), you must walk in the grace of submissive obedience that has been won for you by Christ's own submissive obedience.

When you do, you and your husband display the glory of the gospel in your marriage. Both the church and the world behold in you a vivid picture of the good news of covenant-keeping grace between Christ and His church.

There is no greater privilege than to tell the truth about the gospel by which you have been saved. Walk in the strength of that power.

Study Questions:

1. If someone asked how you would define what a woman is, what brief answer would you give? Why?

2. What great honor is implied in woman's identity as a "helper"? Do you feel honored by that, or is it a struggle? If you feel it's a struggle, how can you remedy that?

3. The chapter claimed that "the foundation of what it means to be woman is to be one who can suitably help a man to walk in obedience to the calling that God has placed on his life." Do you believe that accurately represents biblical teaching? Why or why not?

4. Other than marriage, what are three ways in which all Christians are called to live a life of submission? Support your answer with Scripture.

5. How did Satan's temptation of Eve subvert the created order of headship and submission?

6. What does a wife's joyful submission to her husband communicate about the gospel? What does her lack of submission communicate about the gospel?

7. Write out an example of a way you can respectfully refuse to follow your husband into sin.

8. Read "Its Practical Outworking" again. List three specific ways you personally need to grow in responsive submissiveness. For each, sketch a brief plan for how you'll make improvements over the next four weeks.

9. Write out an example of a way you can respectfully request your husband to excel more in his leadership. Do so in a way that does not undermine his leadership.

11

Feminine Beauty

Modesty and Quietness as Woman's Adornment

THE LAST CHAPTER introduced us to perhaps the most foundational element of a woman's identity: She is to be a helper, one who can suitably help a man walk in obedience to the calling that God has placed on his life. We found that Scripture often characterizes that helpfulness in terms of submissiveness, and we examined the Bible's teaching concerning nine features of biblical submission.

In this chapter, we turn to two more marks of biblical womanhood.

Beautiful Modesty

The second mark of biblical womanhood we'll address is her beautiful modesty. As Peter discussed the Christian's duty of submission after the pattern of Christ (1 Pet. 2:13–25), he called wives to the same instruction: "In the same way, you wives, be submissive to your own husbands" (1 Pet. 3:1).

In verses 3 and 4, he told these women that their beauty had less to do with external adornments and more to do with her inward character: "Your adornment must not be merely external—braiding the hair, and wearing gold jewelry, or putting on dresses; but let it be the hidden person of the heart, with the imperishable [beauty] of a gentle and quiet spirit, which is precious in the sight of God."

Paul commented even more directly when he addressed the women of the church at Ephesus, calling them to beautiful modesty: "Likewise, I want women to adorn themselves with proper clothing, modestly and discreetly, not with braided hair and gold or pearls or costly garments, but rather by means of good works, as is proper for women making a claim to godliness" (1 Tim. 2:9–10).

Beauty

In these passages, both Peter and Paul spoke of the propriety of a woman's adornment. Peter said, "Your adornment must be," and then spoke of "imperishable beauty." Paul said, "I want the women to adorn themselves." So, the apostles are not against a woman's adornment.

We mentioned in the previous chapter that this term, *kosméō,* refers to beautifying something. In Titus 2:10, it referred to how godly submission would adorn the doctrine of God, our Savior. Not that it would make Christian truth more attractive than it is (that's impossible); but that it would contribute to displaying Christian truth to be as attractive as it is. The same is true in the case of a woman's adornment. She is permitted to adorn herself in a beautiful, respectable, modest way.

We see that especially in First Timothy 2:9, where Paul said, "I want women to adorn themselves with proper clothing." Literally, you could translate that, "I want women to order themselves with orderly clothing." This takes effort and preparation. This means it's right for a woman to prepare so that she is dressed in an appropriate, orderly, put-together, beautiful way.

In calling for modesty, neither Peter nor Paul called upon Christian women to ignore their appearance and present themselves in a slovenly, sloppy, or homely manner. This is no call for the proverbial "burlap sack" as an alternative to immodest clothing. John MacArthur observed, "This text [1 Peter 3] does not prohibit wives from styling their hair, wearing jewelry or lovely clothing, which is why the translators added 'merely.' . . . The point is that this was not to be the preoccupation or main concern."[1]

Some people read these passages and conclude that the apostles prohibit all jewelry and hairstyling. But that can't be, because the final phrase of First Peter 3:3 is best translated not as "putting on dresses" (as if to single out a particular kind of clothing), but as "putting on garments"—clothing in general. If this verse prohibited all jewelry and all hairstyles, it would seem to be prohibiting all clothing as well! But that is certainly not the point. Rather, the message is that women should not be so focused on externals that they neglect true beauty, which is internal, above all else.

So, when it's accompanied by modesty and discretion, there is appropriate beauty—even an appropriate external beauty—that a woman displays.

1 John MacArthur, *1 Peter*, MacArthur New Testament Commentary (Chicago: Moody, 2004), 179.

The woman is, in that sense, the beautiful gender. Sometimes she is called "the fairer sex." That's a biblical notion. Back in Genesis 6:2, we read, "The sons of God saw that the daughters of men were beautiful." In fact, the first time the term "woman" was used outside of Genesis 1–3, we're told Sarah was "a beautiful woman" (Gen. 12:11). Rebekah was called beautiful in Genesis 26:7. Genesis 29:17 says, "Rachel was beautiful of form and face." Abigail (1 Sam. 25:3), Bathsheba (2 Sam. 11:2), Tamar (2 Sam. 13:1), and Esther (1:11; 2:7) were all called beautiful.

There is something appropriately beautiful about women. And while the same word is used to describe a handful of men as "handsome," it is noticeably scarce. When the term is used of men, the contexts of those passages seem to indicate that their handsomeness was exceptional.

At the very least, the Song of Solomon teaches us that a husband should find his wife to be beautiful, and he should tell her so. The man called his bride "most beautiful among women" (1:8), and "My beautiful one" (2:10, 13). In several instances, he exclaimed, "How beautiful you are, my darling!" (1:15; 4:1), or "How beautiful and how delightful you are, my love, with all your charms!" (7:6). And in 4:7 he said to her, "You are altogether beautiful, my darling, and there is no blemish in you." It is as if the bridegroom decided that his wife would be the standard of feminine beauty in his mind. Whatever she was, she was beautiful to him.[2]

All of this is to say: beauty is inherent to womanhood in a way that is not quite analogous to manhood. That means there is an appropriate sense in which a woman desires to be lovely—sort of in the same way there is an appropriate sense in which a man desires to be strong. Surely, in both cases, those desires can be perverted into vanity, pride, and self-preoccupation (Isa. 3:16–26; Ezek. 16:1–63). But throughout Scripture, men are exhorted to "act like a man" and "be strong," and then that strength is defined in this biblical sense of being morally steadfast (1 Cor. 16:13–14), and faithful to Scripture (1 Kings 2:2–4).

At the same time, throughout Scripture, women are exhorted to adorn themselves modestly and discretely, and to press after true and proper beauty, which is defined in this biblical sense of a gentle and quiet and submissive spirit. Men, desire to be biblically strong. Women, desire to be biblically beautiful. Something inherent to women makes the pursuit of true beauty distinctly feminine.

---

2 That is a good practice. A husband should cultivate a sense of what is beautiful by looking at the wife God has given him and making her the standard.

Modest

So, women are beautiful. But they are beautifully modest. And you see that emphasis in those same passages.

Both Peter and Paul spoke of a woman's displaying her beauty modestly. Peter was more indirect, saying a woman's "adornment must not be merely external"—that it shouldn't consist merely in hairdos and jewelry and dresses (1 Pet. 3:3).

Paul is more direct, speaking of being adorned "modestly and discreetly" (1 Tim. 2:9).

Some women in the church at Ephesus were prostituting the gathering of the church for worship on the Lord's Day into an opportunity to draw attention to themselves. Whether they were flaunting their wealth by a display of expensive clothing, or flaunting their beauty by dressing in a sexually tantalizing way, they were making the gathering of the saints about them—about satisfying their lust for others' attention and admiration, rather than directing all attention and admiration to the Lord Jesus alone.

There may not be an exhortation that young Christian women need to hear more than these resounding calls to modesty and discretion. America's pornified culture exerts far too much influence on those who name the name of Christ. Too many young Christian women are taking their fashion cues from Instagram influencers rather than from the Scriptures and from spiritually mature, godly women in the body of Christ. It seems grievously evident that, if the besetting sin of the young Christian man is lust, the besetting sin of the young Christian woman is lusting after being lusted after.

But when beauty is perverted like that—even when it's still tantalizing to some—it becomes ugly. Beauty displayed immodestly is ugly: "As a ring of gold in a swine's snout so is a beautiful woman who lacks discretion" (Prov. 11:22).

That's true of women of all ages, but it strikes me that young women especially need to hear this. If you think, ladies, that you have to dress immodestly to be attractive, recognize that the husband you want won't be enticed by the indiscrete flaunting of your beauty.

Yes, young men will value physical attraction. But the godly man—the husband you want—will be attracted to the hidden person of the heart and will actually be more attracted to a woman who displays that inner beauty. If your immodesty attracts a young man, he's not the man you want as your spiritual head. Young men who love Christ and who will lead you well will have trained themselves to flee temptation (1 Cor. 6:18; 2 Tim. 2:22). If your indiscretion becomes an occasion for him to forfeit communion with Christ by yielding to his lusts, a godly young man will be repulsed by immodesty—the way you might recoil from getting too close to a pig's snout, no matter how pretty the ring in it is.

This is not the setting for specifics about what clothes are acceptable or not. But if you're married and wondering whether this or that outfit is immodest, ask your husband. If you're still a young lady living at home, ask your parents—mom *and* dad—especially if they're believers. If you're unmarried and out of the home, and you're unsure about whether you've become more influenced by the world around you than by the Spirit of God in you, ask an older, more spiritually mature lady in the church whose judgment you trust. Elder sisters, be honest with your younger sisters when they ask.

With hopes of being helpful, I'll mention three principles to consider. First, ladies, there are certain things about you that only your husband should know. (Let the reader understand.) Certain women seem to be very fond of sharing that knowledge with others. Don't be one of those women. Don't dress in a way—whatever the context—that lets others know things about your anatomy that only your husband should know.

Second, clothing should be a frame for the face, not the body.[3] The human face is our relational center. When you communicate with someone, you look in a person's eyes. When you speak to others, the thoughts of your soul are expressed through your mouth and perhaps your facial expression.[4] If you were looking at a picture and noticed that I was in the background, you wouldn't point to my shoe and say, "That's Mike!" You might say, "Oh, you can tell Mike was close by because you can see his shoe in the corner, there." But it's not me. But if you saw a picture of my face, you wouldn't say, "That's Mike's face," but "That's Mike." There's a sense in which I am my face in a way that I am not any other part of me. That's why so many passages of Scripture refer to seeking God's face (e.g., Ps. 27:8) and God making His face to shine upon us (e.g., Num. 6:24–26): because there's a real sense in which the face stands for the person.

The face is the relational center of the body. And that means clothing ought to be a frame for the face. It should direct attention to that part of us which mediates wholesome, meaningful relational interaction. Clothing that draws attention away from the face and focuses attention on the body—especially those parts of the body by which wholesome, meaningful

3 Strachan and Peacock, *The Grand Design*, 83.

4 Griffo, *The Beauty of the Binary*, 80.

relational interaction cannot take place except by those who are married—communicates that you are interested in what a godly woman should not be interested in from anyone but her husband. That might not be your intent, but that is what such clothing communicates. And you are called to not be so naïve as to communicate what you don't intend.

The beauty of the body is to be expressed privately, between husband and wife in the covenant of marriage. The beauty of the face expresses the thoughts and intentions of the heart, which are at the center of meaningful fellowship between brothers and sisters in Christ. Let your clothes be a frame for your face.

Third, immodesty is not only about being sexually lascivious or physically enticing. It can be immodest to ostentatiously display your wealth (1 Tim. 2:9; 1 Pet. 3:3). Whether an inappropriate display of beauty or wealth or anything else, at the heart of immodesty is the seeking of distinction. It's looking to stand out. It's drawing attention to yourself rather than drawing attention to God and His glory. Jonathan Edwards said, "It is the nature of spiritual pride to cause [people] to seek distinction and singularity." If your presentation of yourself communicates, "I'm different! Look at me!"—if it causes you to be the center of attention—you're falling afoul of the biblical command to be modest.

John MacArthur captured this delicate balance when he said, "A Christian woman should attract attention to her character, not her clothing. A Christian woman should show by her dress and her demeanor . . . that she has no intent to flaunt her wealth, but that she is in appearance and attitude marked out by a humble heart that is obviously committed to worshipping the living God."[5] Women are to be "properly dressed, in a way that is becoming both to the grace and beauty of a woman and to the purpose and intent of worshipping God."[6] Then, commenting on First Peter 3, MacArthur wrote, "The Lord is most pleased when a believing woman's modest yet thoughtful and lovely adornment reflects the inner beauty [that] Christ has fashioned in her."[7]

In other words, a biblical woman is beautifully modest.

---

5 John MacArthur, "God's High Calling for Women, Part 1," https://www.gty.org/library/sermons-library/54-14/gods-high-calling-for-women-part-1 (accessed December 2023).

6 MacArthur, "God's High Calling for Women, Part 1."

7 MacArthur, *1 Peter*, 180.

Gentle Quietness

A third mark of biblical womanhood is that she has a gentle quietness. I recognize that such a comment is jarring to contemporary sensibilities. But the New Testament places a surprising amount of emphasis on the propriety of the Christian woman's quietness as a corollary of that prevailing disposition of submissiveness that we learned about in chapter 10.

In First Timothy 2:11–12 we read, "A woman must quietly receive instruction with entire submissiveness. But I do not allow a woman to teach or exercise authority over a man, but to remain quiet." Here is that famous instruction where the apostle Paul restricted the role of teaching and exercising authority in the church to the men. While women are encouraged to teach one another and to teach children, they are not to occupy the office of pastor or elder in the church because they are prohibited from teaching and exercising authority over men. Paul bracketed this weighty prohibition with a direction for the woman's quietness.

We see something similar in First Corinthians 14:34–35. As Paul closed a section on the practice of spiritual gifts, he again addressed the role of women in the church: "The women are to keep silent in the churches; for they are not permitted to speak, but are to subject themselves, just as the Law also says. If they desire to learn anything, let them ask their own husbands at home; for it is improper for a woman to speak in church." Other translations have "shameful" or "disgraceful."

That's a striking comment, especially in our day when "female pastors" dominate the evangelical landscape. Paul said women are not even permitted to speak in the corporate assembly, let alone preach every week. Paul didn't say a woman couldn't open her mouth while in the church building. This is not talking about greeting one another, or encouraging one another, or enjoying fellowship with one another. It's talking about having a speaking role in the worship service.

While there's much to be said about First Timothy 2 and First Corinthians 14, both texts contribute to this overall picture of quietness being a mark of a mature Christian woman.

But the main text from which I draw this point is First Peter 3:1–4. After instructing Christian wives to be good helpers—that is, to "be submissive to [their] own husbands" (3:1–2)—and then calling them to a beautiful modesty (3:3), Peter told women their truest beauty consisted in their quietness: "Your adornment must not be merely external—braiding the hair, and wearing gold jewelry, or putting on dresses; but let it be the hidden person of the heart, with the imperishable [beauty] of a gentle and quiet spirit, which is precious in the sight of God" (3:3–4).

He was saying that those external manifestations of beauty (hair, jewelry, fine clothing)—no matter how trendy or fashionable—are temporary, fading, and perishable. But the internal beauty of the hidden person of the heart is imperishable.

This is the same term Peter used to describe the imperishable and unfading inheritance that is reserved in heaven for every believer (1 Pet. 1:4). Peter called women to a kind of beauty that is of the same quality as the heavenly inheritance that is the ultimate hope of everyone who has been born again. This is heavenly, eternal beauty.

And what does this beauty consist in? "A gentle and quiet spirit." "Gentle" is the term *praüs.* It's the same word used in Matthew 5:5, where Jesus pronounced a blessing on the meek, because they'll inherit the earth. It's the same word that Jesus used to describe Himself in Matthew 11:29, when He invited us to take His yoke upon us and learn from Him, for, He says, "I am gentle and humble in heart, and you will find rest for your souls."

John MacArthur describes the word as it's used in First Peter 3 as denoting "a humble and meek attitude, expressed in patient submissiveness."[8] Wayne Grudem says, "It means 'not insistent on one's own rights,' or 'not pushy, not selfishly assertive,' 'not demanding one's own way.'"[9] Another commentator writes that to be gentle in spirit speaks of "an amiable friendliness that [is] contrasted with roughness, bad temper, or brusqueness."[10]

Biblical women have a gentle spirit. They're humble, meek, and patient. They're not pushy, assertive, or demanding. They're amiable, and not rough, brusque, or abrasive.

Then there's the term "quiet" (*hēsúchios*). The commentators say it means to be calm, peaceful, and tranquil. It's the opposite of being restless, rebellious, disturbed, or insubordinate.[11]

A woman who possesses a quiet spirit carries herself in a way that makes her a steadying influence on those around her, rather than being someone

8 MacArthur, *1 Peter*, 180.

9 Wayne Grudem, *1 Peter*, Tyndale New Testament Commentary (Downers Grove, IL: IVP, 2009), 148.

10 Peter H. Davids, *The First Epistle of Peter*, New International Commentary on the New Testament (Grand Rapids: Eerdmans, 1990), 119.

11 Davids, *1 Peter*, 119.

who engenders conflict. She calms a room rather than upsets it. She's not emotionally turbulent, tumultuous, or boisterous.

In fact, the Proverbs use the term boisterous to describe the woman of folly—the adulteress who tempts men to be immoral with her. Proverbs 9:13 says, "The woman of folly is boisterous, she is naïve and knows nothing." And she sits at the doorway of her house, calling to the men who pass by, "Stolen water is sweet; and bread eaten in secret is pleasant" (9:17).

Proverbs 7:11 says the adulteress is "boisterous and rebellious." She tells men that her husband has gone on a long journey, and she's prepared her bed for him, and "Come, let us drink our fill of love until morning" (7:18).

But how is "adulterous" the opposite of "quiet"? Well, it's that same disquiet of emotional turbulence, that inability to bridle one's temper, that inclination that just *has* to vent what's inside, that lack of self-control, and that disquiet that draws attention to oneself.

The Hebrew term for "boisterous" is *hāmāh*, and the lexicons define it as "to be restless, or turbulent," or "to roar."[12] It's used that way in First Kings 1:41, where Joab asks, "Why is the city making such an uproar?" The woman who possesses a quiet spirit isn't uproarious. A quiet spirit is the opposite of the disposition described by that silly song from the '70s in which a woman tells the world to "hear me roar." It's the opposite of the disposition represented by a new book I came across recently, written by a professing Christian woman, entitled, *I Won't Shut Up*. That's the way the boisterous woman speaks. That's the way the woman of folly speaks. That's the way the adulteress speaks. "Hear me roar! I am strong! I am invincible!" But the biblical woman doesn't roar. She isn't imposing, harsh, abrasive, assertive, or loud. She has the imperishable beauty of a gentle and quiet spirit.

"Quiet" is not only the opposite of "boisterous"; it's also the opposite of being contentious. In other words, it's possible to keep your volume low but still miss the mark of a quiet spirit.

Someone who is emotionally turbulent will be involved in a lot of conflict. Someone who has a quiet spirit is peaceful—and not just peaceful but peaceable. She is someone who makes peace, rather than one who stirs strife

---

12 Ludwig Koehler and Walter Baumgartner, eds., *The Hebrew and Aramaic Lexicon of the Old Testament*, rev. Walter Baumgartner and Johann Jakob Stamm, trans. and ed. M. E. J. Richardson, electronic ed., BibleWorks 8 (Leiden, The Netherlands: Brill, 1994–2000).

and thrives on contention.[13] She is easily entreatable, not difficult or self-willed. She's reconcilable and eager to forgive; she does not nurse bitterness or hold grudges.

The Proverbs also say much about the "contentious woman." Solomon said, "It is better to live in a corner of a roof than in a house shared with a contentious woman" (21:9; 25:24).

In Proverbs 21:19, he said, "It is better to live in a desert land than with a contentious and vexing woman." The New English Translation renders that, "a quarrelsome and easily-provoked" woman. Better to live in a desert, deprived of the bare necessities of life, than to live with a woman who is poised for conflict.

In Proverbs 19:13, we find, "A foolish son is destruction to his father, and the contentions of a wife are a constant dripping." Similarly, Proverbs 27:15 says, "A constant dripping on a day of steady rain and a contentious woman are alike." It's like raindrops falling from an overfilled gutter, dripping onto some metal surface over and over and over and over again. All day. A woman who is constantly spoiling for a fight, who's constantly finding fault, who's constantly nagging and picking specks out of your eye is like that. The next verse says, "He who would restrain her," that is, restrain a contentious woman, "restrains the wind, and grasps oil with his right hand" (27:16). If you can't be restrained, you're out of control. You don't have a gentle and quiet spirit.

Why does this book of wisdom—this inspired manual for skilled living—make so much of the contentious woman? Because it's a problem, ladies. It's an area of natural temptation, given your constitution in a fallen world. Just as men are more naturally given to be pugnacious—to express their anger in physical altercation—women are more naturally given to be contentious, to express their anger in social and emotional altercations.

Some people in life—men and women—really seem like they just can't be happy unless they're miserable. It's almost as if they stir up dissension and strife just so they can keep the attention off of their own sin. Sisters, the exhortation of these verses is: don't be one of those people. Don't be the kind of woman of whom it is said, "If mama ain't happy, ain't nobody happy." Or "Happy wife, happy life!" Don't be someone who has to be pacified for peace to be in the home.

Be amiable, entreatable, reconcilable, and peaceable. Be more difficult to offend than you are difficult to please. Let things go. Be quick to overlook a transgression (Prov. 19:11). Be an easy person to get along with.

---

13 Calvin, *1 Peter*, 97n1.

In Titus 2:4–5, Paul instructs the older women to train the younger women "to be sensible, pure, workers at home, kind, being subject to their own husbands." You want to be a kind person, because, if nothing else, you have been shown such lavish undeserved kindness by God in the gospel of Christ, and someone who has been the recipient of such mercy cannot fail to be merciful themselves. Remember, "Blessed are the merciful, for they shall receive mercy" (Matt. 5:7). Commenting on Titus 2:5, MacArthur said, "They are to be gentle, considerate, amiable, congenial, and sympathetic, even with those who are undeserving and unkind to them."[14]

Biblical women aren't abrasive and loud. They're gentle and quiet. Their character, attitude, demeanor, and speech are marked by the inward, imperishable beauty of gentleness and quietness. And it *is* beautiful to know people who are ruled by such a spirit.

Peter's point is: if you want to win your unbelieving or disobedient husband to the truth, the imperishable beauty of a gentle and quiet spirit is so much more attractive than the fading beauty of braided hair and gold jewelry and fine clothing.

Godly men aren't attracted to loud, obnoxious, contentious women. Godly men are attracted to the inner beauty of a gentle and quiet spirit.

Even better, God Himself is attracted to that. First Peter 3:5 says that the beauty of a gentle and quiet spirit "is precious in the sight of God."

If you want nothing else in life, you want God to see you as precious. You want Him to be able to look into your heart and find evidence of His grace, as if He could look upon you and say, "Yes, My Holy Spirit has been here."

If that's your desire, dear sisters, then press hard after the true beauty of a gentle and quiet spirit.

---

14 John MacArthur, *Titus*, MacArthur New Testament Commentary (Chicago: Moody, 1996), 87.

Study Questions:

1. Is it right for a woman to give attention to her appearance, and to desire to be attractive to her husband? Support your answer with Scripture.

2. Rate yourself on a scale of 1 to 10 with regard to modesty in your clothing choices. Ask your husband (or if unmarried, your father) to do the same. Discuss the similarity or divergence of your answers.

3. What do you think about the three principles for modesty listed in the chapter? Do your clothing choices wrongly share anything about yourself with others? Do your clothes draw attention to your face, or your body? In what other ways are you tempted to draw attention to yourself? If married, discuss these answers with your husband.

4. What kinds of clothing are off limits? What kinds of clothing do others think are off limits that you believe are permissible? If married, discuss these answers with your husband.

5. List the many adjectives that appear in the section entitled "Gentle Quietness" (e.g., "pushy," "assertive," "restless," "abrasive," "loud"). How well does each describe you? What are three practical steps you can take to improve?

6. What do you take away from the Proverbs' description of the contentious woman? In what ways, if any, does this describe you? What must change?

7. Would your husband and children say that, "If mama ain't happy, ain't nobody happy"? If so, what can you do to change that impression?

12

Queen of the Castle

The Biblical Woman as Homemaker

A FOURTH MARK OF biblical womanhood is that she is a homemaker. For some, that word conjures images of the 1950s, Mayberry, and a sterilized "golden age" full of stereotypes that have often been manipulated into demeaning women.

A statement like, "A woman's place is in the home" is one such trope, as if a woman is somehow out of line if she were to have a meaningful existence outside her house.

I don't intend to carry over all the baggage associated with certain connotations of the word "homemaker." Instead, I mean it more literally: a biblical woman is a maker of the home—one who has the responsibility of directing all of her energy, creativity, love, and strength toward making the home a pleasant environment in which the needs of her family can be cared for, in which discipleship flourishes, in which hospitality is practiced, and in which the Lord Jesus Christ is honored according to His Word.

We'll consider this reality of the biblical woman as a homemaker under two broad headings. And those are 1) her domain; and 2) her duty.

Her Domain: A Worker at Home

In the first place, the biblical woman's responsibility as a homemaker speaks to her domain. This is the primary sphere of responsibility in which the Lord has placed the woman—the domain in which she is to direct her labors for the Lord's glory.

Several passages of Scripture testify to this. In Titus 2, Paul instructed the older women to be "teaching what is good, so that they may [train] the young women to love their husbands, to love their children, to be sensible, pure, workers at home, kind, being subject to their own husbands, so that the word of God will not be dishonored" (2:3–5).

Women are to be workers at home. The Greek word is *oikourgos*, used only here in the New Testament. Its meaning is clear from the two words that are joined together to make the compound word: *oikourgos* comes from *oikos* ("home," "house") and *ergon* ("work"). The woman is to be a home-worker, or a worker in the house.

The leading Greek dictionary says it means to be carrying out household duties or responsibilities, to be busy at home.[1] When Paul instructed the older women in the church to disciple and train the younger women, he wanted them to be trained to function well in their rightful domain; to be workers at home.

A similar emphasis appears in First Timothy 5, where Paul instructed young Timothy about how the church must serve widows. Having lost their husbands, widows had lost their primary means of financial security. Paul gave Timothy some guidelines for how the church could assess whether a widow's financial welfare is to be covered by the generous support of her church family.

The principle was that if a woman had lost her husband and was of an advanced age where she was not likely to remarry or to be able to care for a family, the church should step in and support her, as long as her character was consistent with godliness. But if a widow was young enough to remarry and care for a family, she should pursue that course, so her needs would be met by her new husband rather than the church.

In that context, Paul said, "Therefore, I want younger widows to get married, bear children, keep house, and give the enemy no occasion for reproach" (1 Tim. 5:14).

If your husband has died, and if you're young enough: pursue marriage, have babies, and keep house. The term is *oikodespotein*, from *oikos* ("house") and *despoteō*, from which we get the term "despot." In English, a despot is one who rules. In Greek, a *despotēs* doesn't bear the same connotation of tyranny or cruelty; it just means a master or a lord. It's the term that's used of the Lord God in several places (2 Tim. 2:21; 2 Pet. 2:1; Rev. 6:10). The woman is to be a master of her home. She is to get married, have kids, and to manage a household.

Now, it's true that the ultimate responsibility for "manag[ing] his own household well" (1 Tim. 3:4) falls to the husband, who is the spiritual leader

1 Frederick W. Danker, Walter Bauer, William F. Ardnt, and F. Wilbur Gingrich, *A Greek-English Lexicon of the New Testament and Other Early Christian Literature*, electronic ed., rev. and ed. Frederick W. Danker (Chicago: University of Chicago Press, 2000).

of the home. But here we learn the authority of the day-to-day management of the household is delegated from the husband to his wife, and she manages the household in subjection to his leadership.

Titus 2:5 says older women are to train the young women to be "workers at home, kind, being subject to their own husbands." So, the work she does at home is subject to her husband's leadership; it does not usurp it.

John MacArthur explains, "The man provides the resources through his labor, and the woman manages them for the care of her husband and children."[2] This is her domain.

Insight from the Curse

While those two passages establish the point, Genesis 3 illustrates this reality in an exceptional way. The sin of Adam and Eve brought God's curse into the world—upon the serpent, the woman, the man, and the creation itself. But God cursed the man and the woman distinctly, in ways that relate to each one's proper domain and sphere of responsibility. He cursed the man with respect to his vocation as a worker of the ground (Gen. 3:17–19), but He cursed the woman with respect to her domestic relationships (Gen. 3:16).

One writer observed, "In appointing the curse for his rebellious creatures God aims at the natural sphere of life peculiar to each."[3]

Another said, "God relates the effect of the curse respectively to that portion of His creation mandate (as already established in Genesis 1 and 2) that most particularly applies to the woman on the one hand and to the man on the other hand."[4]

In other words, God's curse identifies the man's natural, pre-Fall domain as working to sustain his family through breadwinning labor, and it identifies the woman's natural, pre-Fall domain as working to sustain her family through childbearing and nurturing labor.[5] She is to be a helper for her husband and to bear and rear children: a worker at home.

This is the sphere of responsibility that the woman was created to be oriented to. This is her natural domain, the place where God has wisely designed

2 MacArthur, *1 Timothy*, MacArthur New Testament Commentary (Chicago: Moody, 1995), 213.

3 Piper, *What's the Difference?*, 39.

4 George W. Knight, III, "The Family and the Church: How Should Biblical Manhood and Womanhood Work Out in Practice?" in *Recovering Biblical Manhood and Womanhood*, 347.

5 Piper, *What's the Difference?*, 39–40.

for her to flourish most, for her to be most fulfilled, for her gifts and talents to be put to the greatest use for achieving the ends her Creator and Lord has designed for her. It is her home base, her ground zero for ministry, where she employs all her energy and creativity to make the home a place of rest, encouragement, and support for her husband; a place of nurture, safety, and fun for her children; a place of welcoming hospitality for the people of God; and a place of ministry to unbelieving neighbors.

Don't Be Deceived

Our unbelieving, satanic, anti-Christ culture, through the so-called feminist movements of the 20th century, has succeeded in despoiling women of the glory of their God-given role of being masters of the home.

The feminist agenda has duped women into believing that being a homemaker is oppressive—that it strips their rights to have a meaningful existence outside the home like men do, meaning that's derived from pursuing a career. The world scoffs, "Keeping a clean and pleasant home, doing laundry, preparing meals? Don't be a slave to your husband!"

No, pursue your self-worth in the working world, where you can be a slave to somebody else's husband; where you can earn money, which you'll need to pay someone else to raise your children; so the daycare workers and public school teachers can train your kids in the same godless worldview that managed to con you out of your birthright.

To my sisters in Christ, I say: Don't be deceived. Don't trade the glory of your God-given responsibility as a worker at home for the mess of pottage of the work-a-day world.

You reply, "What glory? I change diapers and scrub floors! I break up fights between screaming children and struggle to teach elementary education! I make meals that everyone complains about, only then to have to clean a pile of dishes! Every day is the same! Where's the glory in that?"

You need to hear me: no work in the world is more important than the work you do at home in raising your children to be faithful disciples of the Lord Jesus Christ. I do not have adequate words to express this.

In the first place, children are hardwired by their Creator to seek from you, their mother, the nurturing care and the emotional affirmation that you are uniquely equipped by God to give them by being present in their lives, by being that consistent source of stability and encouragement and affection that a nurturer gives. Fathers should be affectionate with their children, and certainly, children need and seek affection from their fathers. But it's no accident that

Paul compared his "exhorting and encouraging and imploring" the believers to the way "a father would [do with] his own children" (1 Thess. 2:11), and then compared his "fond affection" and nurturing care for the church to "a nursing mother [who] tenderly cares for her own children" (1 Thess. 2:7–8).

There's something manly about exhorting, encouraging and imploring. And there's something womanly about affectionate and tender care. Children need both. A child needs the nurturing affection of his mother—not his babysitter.

No Greater Influence

Beyond that emotional impact, no one in the world exerts a greater influence on a child's life than that child's mother. The hours of a mother's instruction, training, and modeling an example to follow are unrivaled.

I recognize that my responsibility as the head of my household is to take a lead role in discipling my children, but Paul calls the woman the *oikodespotēs,* the master of the house. That's a mastery she exercises in subjection to her husband's authority, as we've seen. But simply by virtue of the time that a father spends working outside the home (to fulfill his God-given role as the primary provider), he will not have the impact on his children's day-to-day development like his wife does.

Moms, your kids learn most of the things they learn simply by watching you, speaking with you, and interacting with you. They learn what it looks like to live in submission to Jesus by watching your example. They learn the priority of prayer and Bible reading from seeing you make those priorities in your life. They learn the value of diligence, hard work, and contentment from watching you go about your duties with joy. They learn what it means to live with conviction as they watch you put God's Word into practice. They learn about how a godly wife interacts with her husband, how she employs her home to extend hospitality, and how she prioritizes the needs of God's people in service and fellowship. And on and on we could go.

Dorothy Patterson, wife of a former theological seminary president, made this observation about her role as a mother: "No one—not teacher, preacher, or psychologist—has the same opportunity to mold minds, nurture bodies, and develop potential usefulness like a mother."[6] She's absolutely right. That's why there's been such a bitter war over the educational system in America. It's why the teachers' unions aim to exert so much authority and why the public school systems want to have drag queen story hour in

6 Dorothy Patterson, "The High Calling of Wife and Mother in Biblical Perspective," in *Recovering Biblical Manhood and Womanhood*, 370.

your elementary school library. Everyone knows that as go the children, so goes the nation. To educate a society is to influence a society.

So, ladies, do you want to change the world? Then raise your children as disciples of Jesus Christ. Raise children who know Scripture, who love and support the local church, who prioritize fellowship with the saints, who evangelize the lost, who conduct themselves according to the fruit of the Spirit, and, most importantly, who passionately pursue communion with Jesus.

If you devote yourself to the ordinary, sometimes mundane, sometimes stressful and thankless duties of working at home, you will shape the next generation of the church of Jesus Christ and the next generation of the citizens of this nation. You will literally be the most influential people on the planet.

Work Outside the Home

Does all this mean women are forbidden to work outside the home? No, not necessarily. But because Scripture places so much emphasis on the home as a woman's domain, that is to be her priority. The responsibilities that come with making and keeping a God-honoring home must be met before she would seek opportunities to work or serve outside the home.

First things first. If, after first things are done, there is time for second things, then by all means, enjoy second things. Working at a Christian ministry, a school, a hospital, or even in a support role at your local church are excellent occupations—as long as they don't take you away from the work Scripture prioritizes for you.

Many times that can be done after the children reach a certain age and the needs of the house aren't as demanding. Often, a young mom can be industrious, like the Proverbs 31 woman, who contributed to the family's finances by "mak[ing] linen garments and sell[ing] them" (31:24), or, "She considers a field and buys it; from her earnings she plants a vineyard" (31:16).

So, a woman can earn money at home through some sort of business, while not taking her away from her primary responsibilities. But it is exceptionally rare that a mother of young children is able to meet all the demands of managing a God-glorifying home while also working outside the home. Being a faithful worker at home is demanding labor, often more so than the work done for a paycheck, which is why the Proverbs 31 woman "girds herself with strength and makes her arms strong" (31:17). A woman must cultivate an appropriate, feminine strength for the work she's called to do.

And it's the rare case when work outside the home doesn't take her away from the duties of God-honoring homemaking.

What about the single woman? On one hand, young, single ladies should aspire to get married to a godly man, to have children, and to manage a God-honoring household. But on the other hand, some single women aspire to marriage and motherhood, and the Lord has not yet seen fit to grant that gift. It is biblically permissible for those sisters to earn a living by working outside their home. And they should to do that work heartily, unto the Lord (Col. 3:23).

At the same time, while the Lord may not yet have given you a husband and children of your own, He has certainly given you family: the brothers and sisters of your local church. He's given you spiritual children, whom it is your responsibility to love, care for, serve, sharpen, and disciple.

He intends for your home to be an instrument of your service to your spiritual family: a place of hospitality; a place of refuge and safety for those who might be in danger or in need; a place where Bible studies are hosted, where meals are shared, where spiritual conversations take place, where prayer meetings are held.

A home used in that way requires homemaking, even if no husband or children live there. It requires, as one single woman put it, "warm, comfortable, aesthetically pleasing surroundings."[7] It still requires that you embrace the home as your domain as a woman. It still requires that you put into practice this command to be a worker at home.

Her Duty: To Love and to Nurture

Just as the biblical woman's responsibility as a homemaker speaks to her domain, it also speaks to her duty within that domain. Titus 2:3–4 says older women are to be "teaching what is good, so that they may [train] the young women to love their husbands, to love their children, to be sensible, pure, workers at home," and so on.

As the biblical woman orients herself to the home as her God-given domain, the focus within that domain is on love. The life of devoted service to which a godly woman is called in being a worker at home can only be fueled by the affection for God in Christ that wells up into the action of benefiting those Christ has given us to serve. She is to love her husband, and she is to love her children.

---

7 As cited in John Piper, "Foreword: For Single Men and Women (and the Rest of Us)," in *Recovering Biblical Manhood and Womanhood*, xxvii.

Loving Her Husband

A godly woman who is a worker at home is to see to it that she loves her husband. Our study of biblical manhood showed that the husband must exercise his headship in a loving manner—after the pattern of the Lord Jesus Christ in His loving service of the gospel (Eph. 5:25).

In Titus 2, we learn that the biblical woman is also a lover. And the pattern remains the same: it is Christ's sacrificial service to His people, though we don't deserve it. Also, a wife's love for her husband must be sacrificial even when he doesn't deserve it.

John MacArthur comments about this love that is to be given from husbands to wives and wives to husbands, saying it "refers to willing, determined love that is not based on a husband's worthiness but on God's command and that is extended by a wife's affectionate and obedient heart. Even unlovable, uncaring, unfaithful, and ungrateful husbands are to be loved. This sort of love of husbands and wives for each other involves unqualified devotedness and is a friendship that is strong and deep."[8]

I know what it is to be a husband who is unworthy of his wife's love, and therefore, I know what a gracious gift it is to be loved in spite of that unworthiness. My wife's display of such undeserved kindness is not only a powerful motivation for my love and service to her; it also motivates me to press harder after holiness in my own life—to stop doing things that make it difficult to love me and to start doing things that will make her job easier.

But the kind of love Paul called wives to isn't just gritted-teeth, clenched-fist sacrifice. No, the command to love your husbands includes *liking* your husbands.[9] It's not just about devoted service; it's also about genuine affection.

I understand that your husband won't always be likable, but you are commanded to cultivate an affection for him. Rather than nitpicking to find things to be discontented with, you are to diligently spy out evidences of God's grace in his life where he's been making progress—for which you're able to offer him encouragement, and in which you're able to delight. The result will be that you don't just love him but that you actually like him. That is not less than what Paul commands in Titus 2:4.

And certainly, such love from a wife to her husband will contribute to a happy home. A wife's love is part of what "makes" her "home" the haven of rest, support, and encouragement for her husband that it must be. But that love will

8 MacArthur, *Titus*, 83.

9 Chris Mueller, *Let the Women Be Women: God's Design for Womanhood and Marriage* (Irvine, CA: Three Sixteen Publishing, 2022), 67.

also express itself in her diligence to make the home in all the other ways that that requires. Out of love for her husband, she will keep a clean and orderly house, so it truly can be a place of rest and refreshment, rather than chaos and disorder. Out of love for her husband, she will faithfully use her gifts to steward their home as a means of extending hospitality to others. Love is the engine for homemaking.

Loving Her Children

Similarly, a godly woman who is a worker at home is to see to it that she loves her children. We spoke earlier of how the Scripture presents the woman fundamentally as a nurturer. There is no more natural expression of that nurturing disposition than in a mother's tender and affectionate care for her children (1 Thess. 2:7). A child should find a unique softness in his or her mother. She should conduct herself with her children in a way that makes them always confident in her sympathy and protection. More than that, MacArthur writes that a mother is to love her children "in every way—practical, physical, social, moral, and spiritual—with a love that has no conditions and no limits."[10]

Perhaps the best illustration of this comes in Proverbs 31, Solomon's depiction of the standard of biblical womanhood. We observe in this passage a picture of a godly woman's duties: a woman who loves her husband and her children, and who is a worker at home.

First, "She opens her mouth in wisdom, / And the teaching of kindness is on her tongue" (31:26). This is an expression of spiritual and moral love for both her husband and her children. When she opens her mouth, she speaks what is consistent with the wisdom of God's Word and with the kindness that Scripture directs us to walk in. She is a counselor of her husband and a teacher of her children in the ways of the Lord.

Second, her love is expressed in her diligence to contribute to the economic well-being of the family: "She looks for wool and flax / And works with her hands in delight" (31:13); "She considers a field and buys it; / from her earnings she plants a vineyard" (31:16); "She makes linen garments and sells them, / and supplies belts to the tradesmen" (31:24).

This speaks to the biblical woman's industry. Far from the notion that "the husband works" and the wife "stays home," the wife is a *worker* at home. She summons all of her creativity and giftedness to find ways to contribute to the financial well-being of the household.

Now, she does not bear primary responsibility for that kind of provision; that burden falls on the shoulders of the husband. Nor does it mean that such

---

10 MacArthur, *Titus*, 85.

endeavors take her away from her other household duties. But none of that means that she sits around watching soap operas or being a busybody on social media all day long. The biblical woman loves her husband and children by being a worker at home, even unto the economic blessing of the household.

Third, "She rises while it is still at night and gives food to her household and portions to her maidens" (31:15). The godly homemaker takes primary responsibility to prepare the meals the family will eat. The father's responsibility as the primary provider is to earn enough money to buy food. But Scripture seems to place primary responsibility on the mother to prepare healthy, nourishing meals for those for whom she is responsible. Providing for their physical needs is one way to express love for her husband and children.

Fourth, "She is not afraid of the snow for her household, For all her household are clothed with scarlet. She makes coverings for herself; Her clothing is fine linen and purple" (31:21–22). The mother is responsible to clothe her household. Now, that looks different for families today than it would have looked in Solomon's era. Today it doesn't require weaving fabrics on a loom or washing clothes in the river. But a legitimate application is that Mom bears primary responsibility to keep the children in clean, presentable, modest clothing. It doesn't mean Dad can't help with the laundry, but that responsibility falls primarily to her.

Given all of that, fifth, the Proverbs 31 woman is strong: "She girds herself with strength and makes her arms strong" (31:17); "Strength and dignity are her clothing, and she smiles at the future" (31:25). Everything we've just spoken about takes strength, stamina, and fortitude. Thus, it's not surprising to learn that an appropriately feminine strength characterizes the biblical homemaker. This does not look the same as the masculine strength that must mark the biblical man, but it is strength nonetheless. A woman may be the weaker vessel (1 Pet. 3:7), but that does not mean she is to be weak. She is to cultivate the strength of character, mind, and body to be able to be a teacher and a counselor, to be a hard worker who contributes, to be the one who cooks, and clothes, and manages the household.

WORDS OF ENCOURAGEMENT

It's no wonder that Proverbs begins with the exclamation that the worth of such a woman is far above jewels (31:10). If you struggle to believe that such a calling is meaningful and significant, I want to assure you once again that it is. Dorothy Patterson wrote:

> Homemaking—being a full-time wife and mother—is not a destructive drought of usefulness but an overflowing oasis of opportunity; it is not a dreary cell to contain one's talents and skills but a brilliant catalyst to channel creativity and energies into meaningful work; it is not a rope for binding one's productivity in the marketplace, but reins for guiding one's posterity in the home; it is not oppressive restraint of intellectual prowess for the community, but a release of wise instruction into your own household; it is not the bitter assignment of inferiority to your person, but the bright assurance of the ingenuity of God's plan for complementarity of the sexes, especially as worked out in God's plan for marriage; it is neither limitation of gifts available nor stinginess in distributing the benefits of those gifts, but rather the multiplication of a mother's legacy to the generations to come and the generous bestowal of all God meant a mother to give to those He entrusted to her care.[11]

Another writer captures it helpfully:

> Every second of such a life matters to God. Doxology is in the details: a woman who sacrifices her own free time, her serious intellectual and vocational interests, and her goals to care for little children, make healthy and tasty meals for her loved ones, organize, manage, and clean a home, express support and love for her husband as he works hard to provide, and teach her progeny the word of God in all its fullness. Such an existence is more than a job conducted within the confines of a home; it is a vocation. It involves the full measure of a woman's gifts, abilities, and talents, and it is not a lesser call than a prestigious out-of-the-home career. In fact, such labor is in general terms far more demanding than paycheck-driven work, for the work of child raising and homemaking means the direct shaping of lives and even eternal destinies.[12]

No matter what the culture says, Mom, your ordinary daily work as a homemaker is extraordinarily significant. Its importance cannot be overstated. Love and embrace that role for the honor that it is. And don't listen to this apostate culture when they tell you different.

LOOKING UNTO JESUS

You may read of Scripture's standard of biblical womanhood and be tempted to despair at how far short you fall of this calling. In a sense, it's right for you to feel that way. This lifestyle is impossible to achieve in the strength of your own willpower. You can only attain it by the working of the Holy Spirit, who dwells in you through your faith in Christ, and who faithfully applies

11 Patterson, "High Calling," 377.

12 Strachan, *Reenchanting Humanity*, 158–59.

all the richness of the spiritual blessings that Christ Himself purchased for you in His atoning death on the cross.

Sisters, if the Word brings conviction for your sinful failures, praise the Lord that the Jesus came not for the righteous but for sinners (Luke 5:32). Raise your eyes to Calvary's cross, where your Substitute bore every one of your failures in His own body, nailed them to the cross, and buried them in Joseph's tomb. "Behold Him there, the Risen Lamb: your perfect, spotless righteousness," the old hymn says, and remember that "while in heaven He stands, no tongue can bid you thence depart."[13]

Look unto Jesus as the perfect embodiment of what He calls you to do. If I can say it without being crass, Jesus is the consummate "homemaker." He "opens His mouth in wisdom," as the wisdom of God incarnate (1 Cor. 1:30), the Word from the Father (John 1:1), and long-expected Prophet who declares God's Word to God's people (John 6:14; Deut. 18:15–18).

He works diligently; His works of obedience are all our righteousness (Matt. 3:15; Rom. 5:18–19). He is the one who worked until the whole of God's wrath was extinguished—until there was no bitterness left in that cup for us to drink (John 19:30; Heb. 2:17).

He provides the choicest food for His household. He is the Bread of Life, who invites us to feed on Him by faith (John 6:35), to taste and see that the Lord is good (Ps. 34:8).

He makes us part of the Father's household; we who were slaves are made to dwell in the household of God where His provision is abundant (Ps 36:8). As to clothing, Christ clothes us in garments of salvation. He wraps us in the robe of His own righteousness (Isa. 61:10). And as for strength, no one was ever stronger than our Champion of salvation, who bore all our sins to Calvary and put them away by bearing their punishment in Himself, so we could be reconciled to God and members of His own household. What a home the Lord Jesus has made for His people!

And that's true for every believer—man, woman, boy, or girl. In every way that we have failed to live up to the standard our Father calls us to, our elder Brother has obeyed perfectly and has satisfied perfectly.

United to Him by faith alone, the spotless robe of His righteousness is draped across your shoulders; His blood washes your stains clean, so that despite your sins and failures, you are forgiven and accepted by the Father.

On that solid foundation of acceptance, remember that Christ is yours not only for justifying righteousness but also for sanctifying righteousness.

---

13 Charitie Lees Smith, "Before the Throne of God Above" (hymn), public domain.

He supplies the power to obey His commands, as He works in you, both to will and to work for His good pleasure. So, wage the war against your sin in the strength of knowing that He has purchased for you and provided the power for you to walk in obedience to Him (Eph. 2:10).

Study Questions:

1. What do the terms *oikourgos* and *oikodespotein* mean for God's design for the woman's domain? How do you feel about that?
2. Describe the balance between a woman being a maker and manager of the home and the husband's responsibility to manage his household well.
3. The chapter claims there is no more important work than the work a mother does at home. Are there any ways in which you struggle to believe this? What are they, and how do you fight against them?
4. What are some ways that working outside the home could interfere with the priorities of making the home?
5. What are some ways that working outside the home would not interfere with the priorities of making the home?
6. What is one way you can grow to be more like the virtuous woman of Proverbs 31? How will you plan to make progress in this area?
7. Do you struggle more with letting your home become disorderly or with being a perfectionist as to neatness? In what ways does that hinder the restfulness and usefulness of your home? How can you improve?
8. If asked, would your husband say that you like him, as well as love him? What is something you can do to convince him?
9. The chapter outlines five practical ways the Proverbs 31 woman loves her children. In which of those areas do you need to grow most? How will you plan to make progress?

13

Learning and Teaching in the Fear of the Lord

The Character of Biblical Womanhood

SO FAR, WE'VE FOUND THAT a biblical woman is a helper, is beautifully modest, has a gentle and quiet spirit, and is a worker at home. In this chapter, we'll consider five more marks of biblical womanhood, describing the kind of woman each sister in Christ should aspire to be as she conducts her life unto the glory of God.

A Learner

A fifth mark of biblical womanhood is that she is a learner. As Paul addressed the woman's role in the local church, he said, "A woman must quietly receive instruction with entire submissiveness" (1 Tim. 2:11). The emphasis is on the submissive manner in which the woman is to attend public worship. In that context, she is to be a learner rather than a teacher, as verse 12 makes abundantly clear.

But embedded in this instruction is a command for the woman to be a learner: "A woman must receive instruction." That is a third-person imperative from the verb *manthanō*, which means "to learn." Literally, the verse says, "Let the woman learn." Even though women are not to teach men in the corporate assembly, "neither are they to be shut out of the learning process," as was often the case in the world of the first century.[1]

The Babylonian Talmud says of the Jewish worship service, "The men came to learn, the women came to hear."[2] But Paul says, "No, let the woman learn!" She is to be a learner.

1 MacArthur, *1 Timothy*, 82.

2 *Hagiga* 3a, as cited in Knight, *The Pastoral Epistles*, 139.

This seems especially relevant in our conservative evangelical circles today, because some are so disgusted by the rampant feminism and egalitarianism in the church that they swing the pendulum. Since so many self-appointed female teachers are drifting into error and leading many astray, some voices suggest that women should not teach other women theology at all, and that therefore they should not concern themselves with learning the depths of systematic theology and church history. Instead, they should focus on devotional reflections and passages they can apply to their domestic responsibilities.

Now, I acknowledge that feminism has ravaged many of the "ministries" of popular female "preachers" and authors. It grieves me to see women's book clubs and Bible studies turn into little more than emotion-driven group therapy sessions. But the remedy for that is not less theology. It's not less of a focus on the deep things of God, on the meaty truths of sound doctrine, on the proper interpretation and application of Scripture. It requires more Bible, more doctrine, and more discernment.

Paul said, "Let the woman learn."

The term *manthanō* is the verb form of the cognate noun *mathētēs*, which is the word the New Testament uses for "disciple" (Matt. 5:1). The heart of that term is the concept of being a learner.

A disciple is one who learns by following a teacher. A woman who is a disciple of Jesus Christ is to be a learner, a disciplined studier and applier of the Word of her God. Her soul is to pant after knowing her God as the deer pants for the water brooks (Ps. 42:1), a longing that resolves itself in studying all of what God has revealed of Himself in the Scriptures.

We need to have done with the vapid, saccharine women's ministry pablum—the sappy, syrupy, "God thinks you're beautiful just as you are" shtick that strokes women's egos but puts no steel in their spines. We need women of conviction, steadfast in the truth of Scripture, who will pass on those convictions to their children and to their younger sisters in the body of Christ.

The theological malnourishment that results from saying, "Let the men worry about theology; just keep telling me how beautiful God thinks I am," produces spiritual twigs that snap under the slightest pressure. We need women who are oaks, solid and steadfast, who can bear the spiritual weight of discipleship, who are examples of patient perseverance under trials, who are composed of a gentle and quiet spirit and are not ruled by emotions, and who can be a source of wisdom and encouragement for their children and for their church.

In the previous chapter, we spoke about how the most influential people on the planet are those who shape the thinking and worldview of the next generation, and how God's design is for that influence to be mediated primarily through mothers. I would hope, then, that women know the Scriptures at least as well as their brothers in Christ do.

Those who spend the most time evangelizing our children should be full of the Word that makes them wise unto salvation (2 Tim. 3:15). Those responsible to equip our children to live wisely and skillfully under the Lordship of Jesus should be drenched in the Proverbs, which teach us how to walk in the fear of Yahweh, the beginning of wisdom (9:10).

Mothers need to be able to explain the dynamics of spiritual change to children—how the heart is tempted by sin because it's promised a satisfaction that never comes, but how the sweetest satisfaction that the heart can know comes from communion with Christ on the path of obedience. Because a woman is to teach her children how to live well in this world, she emphatically needs to be a learner—a disciple of what the God of the world has said, and how it maps onto day-to-day living.

And it's not just for discipling her own children; it's for being a good friend to her sisters in Christ. It's being an instrument of sanctification in the lives of fellow church members, someone to whom younger women can come for counsel. "You've walked with Christ longer than I have. Why can't I find the motivation to be in the Word or in prayer? Why can't I subdue this particular sin in my life? What strategies have you found helpful in rising against temptation and putting off sin and putting on righteousness?" These are questions that only a learner—only a student of the Word—can answer.

So, let the women learn. Let them learn bibliology—not only the contents of Scripture, but the character of Scripture: that it's inspired, infallible, inerrant, authoritative, and sufficient—and all that those terms mean.

Let them learn theology proper—not just the Word but the God of the Word: that He is sovereign, immutable, impassible, self-sufficient, eternal, and infinite; that He is Triune: one essence subsisting in three co-equal, coeternal persons.

Let them learn the person and work of Christ and of the Holy Spirit. Let them learn the doctrines of man and sin, so they can answer, "Who am I, and what has gone wrong with me?"

Let them learn of the great work of atonement—of what really happened on the cross when our Savior died for sinners. Let them learn of the Spirit's work of regeneration—"What does it mean to be born of God?"—

and of sanctification—"How do we put off sin and put on righteousness?"

Let them learn the doctrine of the church: "Why do we do this on Sundays, and what is it supposed to look like?" And let them learn eschatology: "What is the hope that anchors my soul? What do I look forward to receiving from God in the future?"

Sisters, you must be a faithful master of the home. But you can't just study the recipe book and be a sound, mature, Christian woman. You must be a woman of the Word, and so you must be a learner.

A TEACHER

A woman must not only be a learner, but a teacher as well. Alongside her husband, a biblical woman is to train her children in the nurture and admonition of the Lord. Proverbs 6:20 says, "My son, observe the commandment of your father and do not forsake the teaching of your mother." The Proverbs 31 woman "opens her mouth in wisdom, and the teaching of kindness is on her tongue" (31:26). She gives herself to teach her children in the ways of the Lord, so they grow up to be disciples of Jesus Christ.

We see the effect a mother's influence had on Timothy, the protégé of the apostle Paul, one of the most influential figures in Christian history. Timothy knew the saving Scriptures since he was a child (2 Tim. 3:14–15). But how was that? Acts 16:1 says his father was a Gentile, so Timothy probably didn't learn Scripture from him. Paul noted that the sincere faith in Timothy first dwelt in his grandmother Lois and his mother, Eunice, (2 Tim. 1:5). Even when this young man's father was unable to provide him with needed spiritual leadership, God used his grandmother and his mother to bring Timothy to saving faith.

So, moms, teach your children. Don't leave all the spiritual instruction for your husband to impart. It won't look the same, surely. But that day-to-day, when-you-lie-down-and-when-you-rise-up instruction (Deut. 6:7) is so significant. It literally impacts eternity. It shapes your children's souls, because it is the means by which God does His miraculous work of regeneration and sanctification (James 1:18; 1 Pet. 1:23).

But what if the Lord hasn't given you children? I love Elizabeth Elliot's answer. She says the single woman "can have children! She may be a spiritual mother . . . by the very offering of her singleness, transformed for the good of far more children than a natural mother may produce. All is received and made holy by the One to whom it is offered."[3] To sisters

3 As cited in Piper, "Foreword," *Recovering Biblical Manhood and Womanhood*, xxv.

who grieve over not having biological children, take heart in the fact that you can be the mother to spiritual children in the Lord—those younger women who need and long for the very discipleship that Scripture prescribes for us all to engage in.

> Older women likewise are to be reverent in their behavior, not malicious gossips nor enslaved to much wine, teaching what is good, so that they may [train] the young women to love their husbands, to love their children, to be sensible, pure, workers at home, kind, being subject to their own husbands, so that the word of God will not be dishonored. (Titus 2:3–5)

Mature Christian women are to be teaching what is good. That might be surprising to read, since Paul forcefully restricted the role of teaching in the local church to men (1 Tim. 2:12). But this call to teach comes in the context of the older women's discipling the younger women in the church. Older women should teach what is good so that they may *sōphronizō* the younger women. The NASB translates that as "encourage," but it means to cause one to be sensible, sober, or of sound mind. It "refers to helping others cultivate good judgment and sensibilities."[4]

A good translation of this term would be to train: "so that they may train the young women [in the church] to love their husbands, to love their children, to be sensible, pure," and so on. It refers to a kind of instruction that results in holy and godly living, which brings honor to Christ and His Word.

In his book, *Let the Women Be Women*, Chris Mueller explains that *sōphronizō* speaks of "teaching by example so that others will learn beautiful virtues, good habits, godly behavior, and right attitudes."[5]

> The true biblical training described in Titus 2 is not a seminar or a sermon—it is a life-on-life personal relationship and conversation. It's a discussion about how to apply God's Word in a small group of people or even one on one. It usually means a regular time of prayer together, asking for God to work in your life over specific issues like sins you are dealing with and character qualities you are hoping to develop. It is pursuing the goals in Titus 2 with a person or persons holding you accountable to live biblically and Christlike each day.[6]

---

4 MacArthur, Titus, 78.

5 Mueller, *Let the Women Be Women*, 56.

6 Mueller, *Let the Women Be Women*, 60.

Eventually, he summarizes that this kind of training "speaks of more than dumping content; it is sharing a life in order to change a life."[7]

All of that is excellently said. Life in the body of Christ is about cultivating relationships in which younger Christians can live life alongside more mature believers and see examples of faithfulness lived out in front of them. It's easy to come to church, go through the motions, and never really open your hearts and homes to your fellow-believers. It's easy to just blend in with the crowd, and remain anonymous, so no one really knows what things are like at home, between you and the Lord.

The result of that disjointed, disconnected living is perpetual spiritual immaturity. Such a congregation may be well-informed but spiritually stunted, because they've never learned to practice the truths they've been taught.

Contrary to that, Paul teaches that women learn how to be sound, mature, biblical Christian women, not only from hearing biblical femininity preached from the pulpit or explained in books, but from watching sound, mature, biblical Christian women—from seeking their counsel and inviting their correction.

And so, ladies, you must devote yourselves to this kind of life together. Younger women, devote yourselves to seek this kind of discipleship from your elder sisters. Older women, devote yourselves to being a resource—a teacher to the next generation of Christian women in your local church.

Now, it's true that the focus of this teaching is less on academic doctrinal instruction and more on women's duties and responsibilities to their families (Titus 2:4–5). But that practical instruction is grounded in the great doctrines of the faith, the principles of Scripture. All sound living is rooted in and flows out from sound doctrine. Orthopraxy is the product of orthodoxy. In other words, you can't live right unless you believe right. So, all those theological disciplines we spoke about earlier form the solid foundation upon which practically valuable, life-on-life training can be sustained. This means, ladies, that no area of biblical truth is off-limits for your study. You are to be a learner of all of them, so that you can be a teacher—both to your children and to your fellow sisters in Christ.

Eminent in Good Works

A seventh mark of biblical womanhood is that she is eminent in good works. While every Christian should be eminent in good works, several key passages instructing Christian women single out this exhortation to good works.

7 Mueller, *Let the Women Be Women*, 61.

In First Timothy 2, Paul called women to adorn themselves modestly and discreetly, saying their beauty is not to consist in their hairstyle, jewelry, or designer clothing, "but rather by means of good works, as is proper for women making a claim to godliness" (1 Tim. 2:10).

If you are a woman who professes to follow Jesus, your reputation for good works must precede you, and the people of God should recognize your proven record of practical service to the saints—just as readily as we recognize someone's clothing. That is not because you brag; it's because serving God's people is the natural tenor of your life.

In First Timothy 5, Paul gave guidelines for the church to evaluate whether a widow should be financially supported by that local body of believers. One of the criteria for support is that such a woman be eminent in good works: "A widow is to be put on the list only if she is not less than sixty years old, having been the wife of one man, having a reputation for good works" (1 Tim. 5:9–10).

You may never find yourself in this situation, ladies. But if you did, you ought to have conducted your life in such a way that you would qualify for this kind of assistance, even if you never needed it. "Having a reputation for good works" figures prominently in that list of qualifications.

What kind of good works was Paul talking about? He listed several: "If she has brought up children, if she has shown hospitality, if she has washed the saints' feet, if she has assisted those in distress, and if she has devoted herself to every good work" (5:10).

The first is raising children as disciples of Jesus. We addressed this in the previous chapter. If the Lord has given you children, you must view raising them in the nurture and admonition of the Lord as the primary and most meaningful calling on your life.

Second, he mentioned showing hospitality. In Paul's day, the early Christians were always traveling from city to city, bringing the word of the gospel to the known world. Travel was much more laborious and dangerous then, and so these Christian workers would need places to stay and be refreshed. Paul said a Christian woman should have a reputation for opening her home to facilitate that kind of ministry.

While it might not look exactly the same today, the principle still applies: A godly woman uses her home as the ground-zero of her ministry labors, whereby she helps to refresh and meet the needs of the saints. Hospitality means keeping such an orderly, welcoming, functioning home that it becomes a home-base or a hub for service to the body of Christ.

The text doesn't say the home must be spotless, spacious, or outfitted with the most fashionable décor. It just has to be hospitable; an orderly, functioning, and welcoming house, where the saints' needs can be met.

Third, Paul spoke of washing the saints' feet. In that day, people often walked barefoot or with open sandals along the dusty roads of the ancient Near East. Consequently, foot washing was no pleasant endeavor, a task often given to the slaves. Few acts of service were humbler than this, which is why it was such an astonishing display of humility for the Lord Jesus to do it (John 13:1–11).

Eventually, "washing the saints' feet" became a euphemism for someone with a humble spirit of service after the pattern of the Lord Jesus—someone willing to devote himself to the most menial, dishonorable, inconvenient works of service. Paul says this should mark the biblical woman.

Fourth, He spoke of assisting those in distress. This is a woman who, when she learns of a brother or sister in affliction, feels that affliction as if it were her own. She enters into that affliction herself and does all she can to relieve the pressure it causes. That might mean being a good listener, offering encouragement and exhortation, or even meeting a financial need.

Not long ago, a member of our church said she was afraid for the safety of herself and her two children and needed to leave her house for the night. I called another couple who lived near her and had space for a few guests. The couple had young kids and the wife was six months pregnant. But when the woman heard of her sister's distress, she bore the inconvenience and opened her home to these three fellow believers, helping them until they made other arrangements. That's the kind of thing Paul was talking about.

Are you that kind of woman who devotes herself to her family? Do you bear with inconveniences and welcome the most difficult and humble service? Do you manage a home that's ready to become a haven to others? Do you feel the needs of the saints as your own? That's a mark of a biblical woman.

SOUND IN SPEECH

An eighth mark of biblical womanhood is that she is sound in speech. Titus 2:3 says, "Older women likewise are to be reverent in their behavior, not malicious gossips nor enslaved to much wine." James said, "No one can tame the tongue; it is a restless evil and full of deadly poison" (3:8). He called the tongue "a fire, the very world of iniquity" (3:6). Jesus Himself said we will give account for every careless word we speak (Matt. 12:36–37). Just as young men can tend to be careless with our words (Titus 2:6–8), women can also be beset by the temptation to gossip.

"Not malicious gossips" is literally translated, "not devils." It's the word *diabolos*, which is used more than thirty times in the New Testament to refer to Satan (e.g., Matt. 4:1; 25:41; John 13:2).

The term literally means "slanderer," fitting for Satan, who is a liar and the father of lies (John 8:44), the "accuser of [the] brethren . . . he who accuses them before our God day and night" (Rev. 12:10). *Diabolos* characterizes Satan himself, and it's the term Paul chose for those who engaged in the sin of gossip.

Paul warned elsewhere against this behavior: "At the same time they also learn to be idle, as they go around from house to house; and not merely idle, but also gossips and busybodies, talking about things not proper to mention" (1 Tim. 5:13).

It seems the older women in Crete, and perhaps the younger widows in Ephesus, had more time on their hands than they knew what to do with. Rather than using their time constructively, they passed the time concerned about issues that were none of their business. It's a short walk from being that kind of busybody to gossip, and a short walk from gossip to the kind of slander—the defamation of character and reputation—that marks the enemy of our souls.

That should sound familiar in our generation of social media: scrolling through everyone's business, remarking about their pictures, envying their vacations, complaining about their tweets. It can even mask itself in the guise of righteousness: "I'm just using social media to refute false doctrine!" But before you know it, a woman becomes a keyboard warrior, rebuking people she has no responsibility for, while neglecting the responsibilities she does have to care for her husband, her children, her home, and her church.

Do you really have time, sister, to police evangelicalism's errors on the internet, while you have so much discipleship to do in your own home, in your own church, and in your own heart?

Eventually that behavior descends into gossip and slander, and all kinds of defamatory remarks are spread—many times about sound brothers and sisters in Christ.

This should not be. Scripture says the biblical woman recognizes that "A good name is to be more desired than great wealth" (Prov. 22:1), and that therefore, "Death and life are in the power of the tongue" (Prov. 18:21), because a loose tongue can destroy a good name with great ease.

That's why Proverbs 11:9 says, "With his mouth the godless man destroys his neighbor," and it's why Leviticus 19:16 identifies slander as acting against your neighbor's life. A godly woman refuses even to listen to—let alone participate in and perpetuate—the demeaning of others.

As Proverbs 31:26 says, she "opens her mouth in wisdom, and the teaching of kindness is on her tongue." Her mouth is so filled with the praises of her Savior (Phil. 4:8) that she has no time to drag her brothers and sisters through the mud. Her gentle and quiet spirit restrains her from using her tongue to tear down rather than build up (1 Pet. 3:4; Eph. 4:29–32).

FEARER OF GOD RATHER THAN THE FUTURE

Finally, the biblical woman is marked by the fear of God, rather than the fear of the future. Proverbs 31:30 says of the virtuous woman, "Charm is deceitful and beauty is vain, but a woman who fears Yahweh, she shall be praised." The biblical woman is a God-fearer, worshipping and revering God above all else. His Word is the rule of her life. His will is the mandate for her ministry. His glory is the great preoccupation of her soul.

One result of that fear of God is that "strength and dignity are her clothing, and she smiles at the future" (Prov. 31:25). The ESV says, "She laughs at the time to come." Because her faith and her hope are in God and His promises, she looks forward even to what is uncertain with a calm and settled joy.

That kind of attitude steadies the home. When Mom is frazzled, anxious, and frenetic about the uncertainties of days to come, the rest of the house tends to follow suit. The children spend most of their time with her, and so they tend to imitate her demeanor; and Dad often spends time anxiously trying to ease his wife's anxiety.

But when Mom is calm, happy, and joyful—when she smiles at the future, not afraid of anything because of her trust in her sovereign God—the children tend to imitate that settled and happy confidence, and Dad delights in his virtuous wife, whose worth is far above jewels.

In First Peter 3, Peter called wives to be submissive, even when their husbands were disobedient to the Word, urging them to be chaste, respectful, gentle, and quiet. In the next verses, he continued,

> For in this way in former times the holy women also, who hoped in God, used to adorn themselves, being submissive to their own husbands; just as Sarah obeyed Abraham, calling him lord, and you have become her children if you do what is right without being frightened by any fear. (1 Pet. 3:5–6)

What sense does that make? Well, we all understand that the call to submission—especially when a husband is an unbeliever—can tempt even godly women to become fearful. "If I submit myself to this man who isn't even obedient to Christ, he'll run right over me! He'll make me a doormat! I'll be miserable!"

"If I really give myself to this unfettered pursuit of biblical femininity—being a helper, pursuing modest beauty, cultivating a gentle and quiet spirit, being a worker at home—if I really surrender my own identity and who I've always thought of myself to be, I'll lose myself! I'll be vulnerable! And what if I don't find it fulfilling and pleasant and all the things you say it is?"

Peter says, "Dear sisters: there is no reason to fear the future if you fear the Lord." If obedience to the Lord's command to embrace your womanhood leads you to difficult submission, trust the Lord enough to let fear be banished from your heart.

Trust in your God—that His Word will never lead you away from His blessing—and concern yourself with doing what is right. Don't fear; trust God. As John Piper summarized:

> The presence of hope in the invincible sovereignty of God drives out fear. Or to say it more carefully and realistically, the daughters of Sarah fight the anxiety that rises in their hearts. They wage war on fear, and they defeat it with hope in the promises of God. . . . A Christian woman does not put her hope in her husband, or in getting a husband. She does not put her hope in her looks or her intelligence or her creativity. She puts her hope in the promises of God. . . . She laughs at everything the future could bring because she hopes in God. She looks away from the troubles and miseries and obstacles of life that seem to make the future bleak, and she focuses her attention on the sovereign power and love of God who rules in heaven and does on earth whatever he pleases (Ps. 115:3). She knows her Bible, and she knows her theology of the sovereignty of God, and she knows his promise that he will be with her and will help her and strengthen her no matter what. This is the deep, unshakable root of Christian womanhood."[8]

The path of obedience will not always be easy. It will not always bring comfort, ease, and worldly prosperity. But the path of faithfulness to God's design in your femininity *will* bring fellowship with Jesus, who knew what it was to suffer for righteousness' sake (1 Pet. 4:1; Phil. 3:10), and to subject Himself even to wicked men for the sake of faith-filled obedience to His Father's plan (Heb. 12:3).

---

8 Piper, *This Momentary Marriage*, 97.

Though it meant Gethsemane, Golgotha, and even being forsaken by His Father, He set His face like flint to go to Jerusalem, determined to accomplish your redemption. "For the joy set before Him He endured the cross" (Heb. 12:2). He feared the Lord above all else, and He smiled at future that He could see by the eye of faith, one that would restore to Him the glory which He had with the Father before the world was (John 17:5).

"For the joy set before Him He endured the cross, despising the shame." Will the faithful follower of Christ find shame on the path of obedience? If so, she will despise that shame, just as her Lord did. She will think nothing of that shame and will look ahead to the glory to be revealed in us, to which the sufferings of this present time can't compare (Rom. 8:18). She will smile at her future, because her future is with Him.

Study Questions:

1. What resources can you procure to grow in your understanding of biblical doctrine? Ask your husband if you could study a systematic theology text together.

2. Name a mature woman in your church whose life you can observe as an example of biblical womanhood. Name a younger woman in your church whom you can invite to observe your life. Over the next four weeks, take steps to build these discipleship relationships.

3. Assess your competence in (a) raising children as disciples of Jesus, (b) showing hospitality, (c) offering humble service, and (d) assisting those in distress. Pick one area in which to grow, and list practical steps for making progress.

4. Just between you and the Lord, list three ways you have recently participated in the sins of gossiping and/or being a busybody. Confess, repent, and seek forgiveness. Note any patterns and determine what you must do to put away sins of speech.

5. List at least three things that make you fearful. What promises does God make to you that help you fight those fears?

6. How does the example of Christ give you courage to embrace your role of submission without fear?

Conclusion

THE WORLD AROUND US is in utter confusion. But as we have set our minds on the things above, looking into the pure fountain of God's Word, we have found divine truth to be the remedy for a culture in chaos.

The Remedy for a Culture in Chaos

Men and women are not autonomous self-creators, free to forge our identities as we see fit. Rather, we are creatures of Almighty God, made in His image, designed to reflect the character of our Creator to the world He has made. Therefore, we receive our identity from Him as a gracious gift, and we live in accordance with His commands.

Gender is foundational to the identity we receive from our Creator, for "in the image of God He created him; male and female He created them" (Gen. 1:27). Our bodies, therefore, are not malleable "meat skeletons" that are merely incidental to our identity. They are instead the kind revelation of God to us, fashioned with care by God Himself, and objective testimony to who we are at a fundamental level.

Therefore, men glorify God by honoring His good design when they look, speak, and behave like men, and women glorify God by honoring His good design when they look, speak, behave like women. Any contravention of this is a rebellious assault on the good design of our loving Creator.

Homosexuality is a species of such a rebellious assault. Marriage was designed by God to be a display of the covenant-keeping grace between our Savior and His bride, the church (Eph. 5:32). Marriage exists, then, as a parable of the gospel, in which the husband is to conduct himself in a way that tells the truth about Christ's relationship with the church, and in which the wife is to conduct herself in away that tells the truth about the church's relationship with Christ. A "marriage" of two husbands would speak of a gospel with two saviors and none saved. A "marriage" of two wives would picture a gospel with two sinful peoples and no savior. Neither is good news; neither is the message that brings forgiveness and salvation. And it is not loving, but hateful, to pretend otherwise.

It's not only homosexual behavior that falls short of God's righteous standard; homosexual desires do, too. Same-sex attraction is not merely a sinless disorder resulting from the curse. Because it is sin to be attracted to what is sinful, same-sex attraction is itself sin to be confessed, repented of, and put to death by the power of the Holy Spirit.

Christianity is above all else a religion of the heart, concerned not merely with conforming our outward behavior to an external standard, but most ultimately with the renewal and renovation of the heart and soul, which conforms us to holiness from the inside out. The gospel provides such reorienting freedom, and those who struggle with same-sex attraction are served best not when we define their sins away, but when we deliver them to the fullness of the gospel's power to sanctify.

If men glorify God when they act like men, and women glorify God when the act like women, then the Bible's teaching on manhood and womanhood—true masculinity and femininity—are of paramount importance.

We found that a biblical man takes the burdensome responsibility of leadership, that he leads lovingly and sacrificially, and that he provides for and protects those under his charge, both physically and spiritually.

The man is to be strong, morally and physically. He is to be sensible, a thinker, dialed in and not aloof, self-controlled, and sexually pure. He is to be dignified, affected with the gravity of living a godly life in a fallen world, full of joy without being goofy or unserious.

He is to be doctrinally sound, delightfully disciplined to study the truth of God and teach it to those he leads. And he is to be sound in his speech, bridling his tongue, putting away foul language, complaining, gossip, and lies—ensuring that whatever he says builds up and gives grace according to the need of the moment.

Correspondingly, we found that a biblical woman delights to be a helper, suitable to assist a man to walk in obedience to the calling God has placed on his life. She embraces the beauty of joyful submission, yielding her gifts and strengths unto the benefit of her husband and children, happily responding in submission to her husband's leadership. The woman pursues true beauty, desiring to be appropriately lovely, eschewing immodesty and drawing attention only to the grace and goodness of Christ.

A biblical woman possesses a gentle and quiet spirit; she is not loud, assertive, demanding, or abrasive. She is eager to make peace rather than to stir strife and contention, easily entreated, and ready to forgive.

The biblical woman is also a maker of her home, employing all her energy and creativity to make the home a place of rest, nurture, safety, hospitality, and ministry. She does not allow even other lawful pursuits to take priority over her management of the home. She is a learner of the truth, and a teacher of the truth to her children and to her fellow sisters in Christ.

She is eminent in good works and sound in her speech, building up rather than tearing down. And because she fears the Lord above all else, happily trusting in His sovereign rule, she does not fear the uncertain future, but smiles expectantly at the grace to come from her loving Father.

GOSPEL STRENGTH FOR GOSPEL LIVING

That is the remedy to a world drowning in self-inflicted chaos and absurdity. God is gracious to make our task clear for us. But clear though it may be, it is not easy.

Those enslaved to transgenderism, homosexuality, or same-sex attraction may despair at the thought that God calls them to be something so radically different than what they feel themselves to be.

Christian men observe how far short their practice falls of their divine calling, and they wonder if they can live up to the standard God lays before them. Christian women, likewise, lament their own failures, fearing they cannot be all that God called them to be as godly women. The answer to these fears is the grace of God in Christ Jesus our Lord.

The Christian life is a lifestyle that is impossible to achieve in the strength of your own willpower. You simply cannot fabricate this kind of Spirit-filled, grace-produced life of sacrificial headship (men) or humble helpfulness (women). It can only be wrought in you by the power of the Spirit of God, who dwells in you, and who applies all the richness of spiritual blessings that Christ Himself purchased for us in His atoning death on the cross.

Dear Christian, if hearing of this standard causes you to be convicted over the ways you miss the mark of biblical manhood or womanhood, raise your eyes to the cross of Calvary, where your Savior, bore every last one of your failures away.

In every way that you have failed to live up to the standard your Father calls you to, your elder Brother has obeyed perfectly and has satisfied perfectly. Because you are united to Him by faith alone, the spotless robe of

His righteousness is draped across your shoulders, and His purifying blood covers the doorposts of your heart, so that despite your sins and failures, you are forgiven and accepted by the Father.

And because Christ is no half-Savior, He is not only yours for justifying righteousness, but for sanctifying righteousness, too. He supplies the power to obey His commands as well, as He works in you, both to will and to work for His good pleasure (Phil, 2:12–13).

And so, wage the war against your sin in the strength of knowing that everything He has called you to, He has purchased for you and provided the power for you to walk in (Eph. 2:10). The progress may be slow and discouraging at times. But fight the good fight of faith; take hold of the eternal life to which you were called (1 Tim. 6:12).

A Call to the Unconverted

To those outside of Christ, you are welcome to this same Savior, who lived, and died, and rose again in the place of sinners, who accomplished righteousness and quenched the wrath of God for all who repent and trust in Him alone for salvation. Confess your sins and failures to measure up, turn from sin and self, and find true life in Christ alone, by believing in Him for all your righteousness.

Dear reader, whether you are man or woman, homosexual or heterosexual, same-sex attracted or some-other-sin-attracted, you have broken the law of Almighty God (Rom. 3:23). As a result, you are a debtor to His justice. Scripture says the wages of sin is death (Rom. 6:23). The penalty for disobeying infinite holiness is infinite punishment: the eternal death of everlasting fire in hell (Matt. 25:41, 46; 2 Thess. 1:9).

Because God is good and holy and just, He will insist that lawbreakers who deserve death receive their just punishment (Exod. 34:7), which means you will go there unless you can offer something to satisfy the infinite justice of this righteously offended God.

But there's nothing you can offer. His righteous standard is so out of reach, and your sinfulness is so pervasive in you, that nothing you could offer Him could pay this debt you owe. Scripture says the best of our righteous deeds are nothing but filthy rags to a God who is this holy (Isa. 64:6).

The good news is that a sufficient ransom payment has been made (Mark 10:45). The Lord Jesus Christ—fully man, and so able to stand in your place, and fully God, and so able to bear your curse—has stood in the place of sinners and has become a curse for us (Gal. 3:13), by dying upon the cross of Calvary, and bearing in His own person all the fullness of God's wrath against the sins of His people (1 Pet. 2:24).

The very wrath that stands ready to break over your head the moment you pass from this life, the Son of God has quenched by His own self-sacrifice (Rom. 3:24–26). He bore the fury of the punishment you deserved to experience for eternity in hell and satisfied the justice of God in three terrible hours (John 19:30).

Dear sinner, He died for sinners, just like you and me. Because He Himself was sinless, because His righteousness is infinite, and because His sacrifice was perfectly acceptable, on the third day after His death on the cross, He rose from the grave in victory over sin and death (Luke 24:5–6), certifying that eternal life now lay in His hands to dispense as He wishes (John 5:21; Acts 17:31).

His promise is that all who turn from their sins and put their trust in His righteousness alone to avail with them before the bar of God's justice will be saved, will have their sins forgiven, their stains washed away, their eternity changed from death to life, from hell to heaven (Rom. 4:4–5; 10:9).

Don't wait another day. Confess your sins, come to Christ by faith alone, and lay hold of eternal life.

CLC
PUBLICATIONS
Fort Washington, PA 19034

This book is published by CLC Publications, an outreach of CLC Ministries International. The purpose of CLC is to make evangelical Christian literature available to all nations so people may come to faith and maturity in the Lord Jesus Christ. We hope this book has been life changing and has enriched your walk with God through the work of the Holy Spirit. If you would like to know more about CLC, we invite you to visit our website:

www.clcusa.org

To learn more about the remarkable story of the founding of CLC International, we encourage you to read

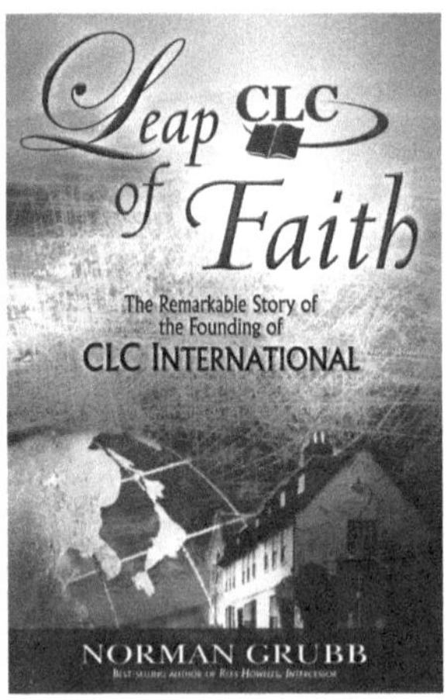

LEAP OF FAITH

Norman Grubb
Paperback
Size 5¼ x 8, Pages 248
ISBN: 978-0-87508-650-7
ISBN (*e-book*): 978-1-61958-055-8